GW00793115

World History
in the
Twentieth Century

U.S.A. AND RUSSIA

P. J. Larkin, M.Sc., B.A.

HULTON EDUCATIONAL PUBLICATIONS LIMITED

© *P. J. Larkin, 1968*

ISBN 0 7175 0063 2

First published 1968
Reprinted 1974
Reprinted 1977
HULTON EDUCATIONAL PUBLICATIONS LTD.
Raans Road, Amersham, Bucks
Printed Offset Litho in Great Britain
by Cox & Wyman Ltd.
London, Fakenham and Reading

Contents

List of Plates

List of Maps, Illustrations and Charts

Preface

This series on World History in the Twentieth Century is divided into four books: Book 1 *The U.S.A. and Russia*, Book 2 *The Far East, Japan, China, India, South East Asia*, Book 3 *The Middle East and Africa*, Book 4 *Europe and World Affairs*. Each book is complete within itself but the four books make a continuous story of World History, 1870–1965.

It is hoped that the contemporary nature of the material, the regional and biographical treatment together with the very full emphasis on maps, diagrams and pictures, will make the series a valuable help for the teacher dealing with the growing number and wider range of pupils staying on at the top end of every type of secondary school.

The books give the teacher the choice of using the material in several ways:

(*a*) A complete world survey, 1870–1965, based on a two-year course
(*b*) A study of a specific region or number of regions
(*c*) A biographical study of world leaders in the 20th century
(*d*) A source of reference to give meaning to current affairs
(*e*) A background to discussion and writing for a General Course in the sixth form
(*f*) A series of project studies: the new nations of Africa, the two world powers, U.S.A. and U.S.S.R., the pattern of change in the Far East, struggle in South East Asia, Nationalism in the Middle East, the Cold War, international government, the League and U.N.O., changing Europe, the impact of world war on the 20th century

A full programme of work and reading is provided for each section of study. The work set for the pupils has been graded at three levels of difficulty. Pupils in the fourth or fifth year of a secondary course should be able to manage all or some of the work under sections *A* and *B*. Questions set under section *C* are intended for pupils in their sixth or seventh year of study.

P. J. L.

The U.S.A.

1. Introduction

The British in America

The foundation of the American nation was laid by British settlers who built up Thirteen Colonies on the eastern seaboard of North America between 1607 and 1733. The colonies stretched from New Hampshire in the north to Georgia in the south. Between 1775 and 1783 the American colonies rose in revolt against Britain and under the leadership of George Washington they won recognition as an independent nation.

THE GROWTH OF THE U.S.A. 1

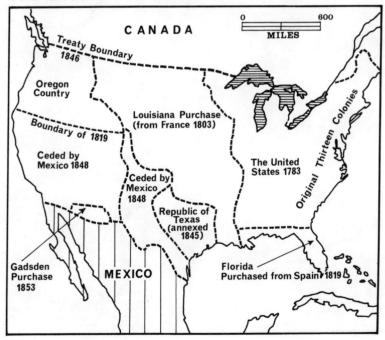

THE GROWTH OF THE U.S.A. 2

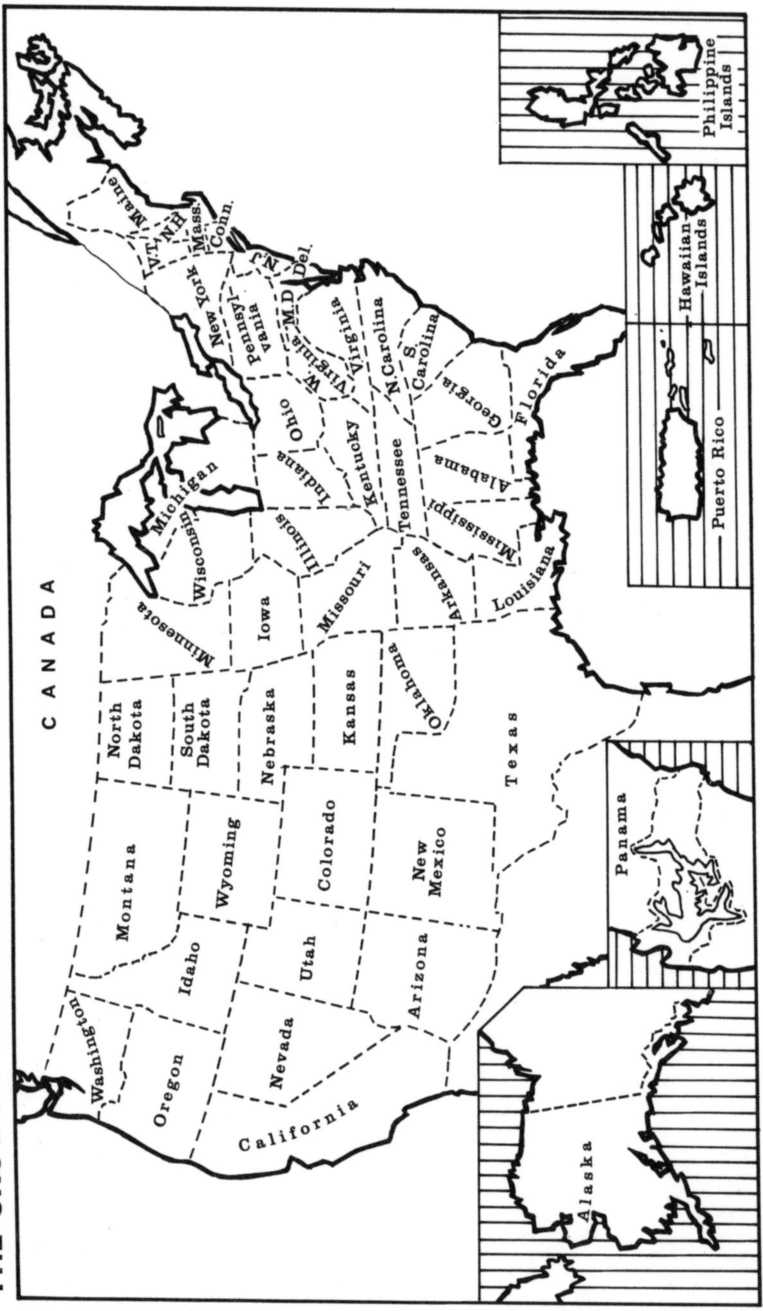

CANADA

Maine
VT. N.H.
Mass.
Conn.
New York
Pennsyl-vania
R.I.
N.J.
Del.
M.D.
W. Virginia
Virginia
N.Carolina
S. Carolina
Georgia
Florida

Michigan
Ohio
Kentucky
Tennessee
Alabama
Mississippi
Louisiana

Wisconsin
Indiana
Illinois
Missouri
Arkansas

Minnesota
Iowa

North Dakota
South Dakota
Nebraska
Kansas
Oklahoma

Washington
Montana
Idaho
Wyoming
Colorado
New Mexico
Texas

Oregon
Nevada
Utah
Arizona

California

Philippine Islands

Hawaiian Islands

Puerto Rico

Panama

Alaska

The American Constitution

One of the first tasks which the Americans had to tackle was to set up a new government for themselves and this was done by 1790. The thirteen states joined together in a Republic. Each state kept its own local government but also accepted the authority of the new Federal government set up to defend and look after the interests and welfare of the union of thirteen states. The constitution accepted in 1790 by a small nation of thirteen states is basically the same today for a nation of fifty states which has become one of the wealthiest and most powerful nations in the world. The United States flag still carries the thirteen stripes for the original thirteen colonies, with a star for every state in the Union. New stars have been added as the Americans have spread across their great continent and brought new states into their Union.

The Congress or Parliament

The Federal government has the right to make laws affecting all the individual states in matters of finance and taxation, inter-state and foreign trade, national defence and general welfare. The Parliament or Congress consists of a Senate to which each state sends two Senators and a House of Representatives elected by the people of each state, on the basis of one Representative for approximately each 300,000 people in the state. A Senator is elected for six years and a Representative for two years.

The President

The President is the Head of State. He runs the whole government in co-operation with his Cabinet of Ministers, his special advisers and with Congress. He is the Commander-in-Chief of the Armed Forces. He appoints all the chief officials of government. He directs the home and foreign policy of the country. The President is elected for a period of four years but can be re-elected for one additional term of four years.

Every law must be passed by a majority in Congress and signed by the President, who can, however, refuse to sign Bills

THE GOVERNMENT OF THE U.S.A.

The White House

Washington D.C.

THE PRESIDENT

Head of State —————

Head of Government

C-in-C Armed Forces   **Elected for 4 years**   Chooses **Cabinet and Advisers**

Working with **Cabinet** and **Congress** he directs home and foreign policy

The Capitol Building   *Washington D.C.*

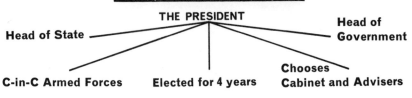

THE SENATE
100 Senators
2 from each State
Senator serves 6 years
One-third of Senate ————— CONGRESS —————
seeks re-election
each 2 years
Deals with vital
national affairs

The
Law-making
body

HOUSE C REPRESENTATIVE
437 Congressm
1 per 300,000 pop. appro
Representati
serves 2 yea
New election for who
House every 2 yea
Deals with mo
local State affa

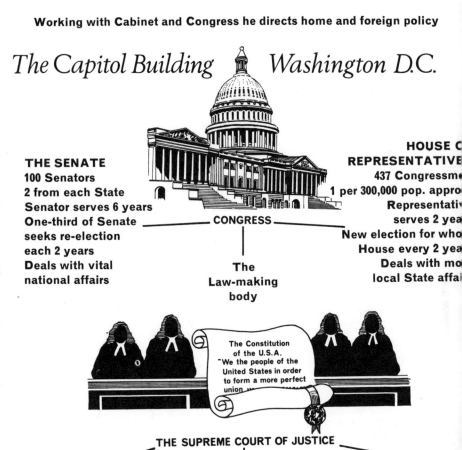

The Constitution
of the U.S.A.
"We the people of the
United States in order
to form a more perfect
union ...

THE SUPREME COURT OF JUSTICE

Nine judges   **Chosen by Presid**

The 'watchdog' of the Constitution

Its decisions have the full force of law

that come to him from Congress. If, however, the Bill after further discussion is passed by a two-thirds majority in Congress then it automatically becomes law.

The President is elected by the individual states. The number of votes which each state can cast in the Presidential election is decided by adding the number of its Senators, which will be two, to the number of Representatives it has a right to send to the House of Representatives. The final number will therefore depend on the size of the population of the individual state. New York, California, Pennsylvania, Illinois, Ohio and Texas have an important influence in a Presidential election because of their high population.

The President is finally chosen by the Presidential Electors from each state in December. It is customary for them to choose the candidate who won the majority of votes in their state in the November election, in which all people over 21 have a vote, and can vote for the Presidential candidate they prefer, together with a long list of state officials.

A Vice-President is elected at the same time and in the same way as the President. He takes over the office of President in the case of the illness or the death of the President until the four-year term is completed. In recent years Truman took over from F. D. Roosevelt and Johnson from Kennedy.

THE NEW YORK TIMES, THURSDAY, NOVEMBER 5, 1964.

Presidential Electoral Vote Distribution in the 50 States and the District of Columbia

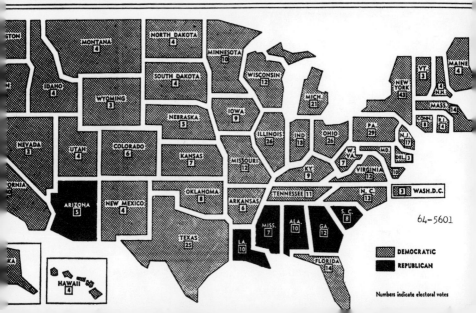

1   Voting procedure in an American election

The Supreme Court

The Supreme Court of Justice, which consists of a Chief Justice together with eight Associate Justices, can decide disputes between states, between American citizens, between Americans and foreigners. One of its major tasks is to see that the government governs in accordance with the Constitution of the U.S.A. as written down in 1790 together with the amendments to that Constitution which have been made in the succeeding years. A majority decision of the Supreme Court has the full force of law throughout the United States.

The Political Parties

For the last hundred years two major political parties have dominated the American political scene: the Republican Party

PRESIDENTIAL ELECTIONS, 1944-64

Year	Candidate	Party	Popular Vote	Electoral Vote
1944	Roosevelt	Democrat	25,602,505	432
	Dewey	Republican	22,006,278	99
1948	Truman	Democrat	24,045,052	304
	Dewey	Republican	21,896,927	189
				(38)
1952	Dwight D. Eisenhower	Republican	33,936,234	442
	Adlai E. Stevenson	Democrat	27,314,992	89
1956	Dwight D. Eisenhower	Republican	35,590,472	457
	Adlai E. Stevenson	Democrat	26,022,752	73
				(1)
1960	John F. Kennedy	Democrat	34,221,463	303
	Richard M. Nixon	Republican	34,108,582	219
				(15)
1964	Lyndon B. Johnson	Democrat	43,121,085	486
	Goldwater	Republican	27,145,161	52

Note 1. Only the two leading Candidates have been included above. Electoral votes cast for other candidates have been put in brackets e.g. (38). The total Electoral Vote is made up by adding the number of Senators (100) to the total number of members of the House of Representatives. The latter figure changes slightly over the period because of changes in population.

Note 2. Number of Electoral Votes varies from State to State on population basis: New York 43 (16·7 million), California 40 (15·7 million), Texas 25 (9·5 million), Nevada 3 (285,278).

Note 3. **Popular Vote** In the November of the Presidential election year there is an election in each state in which all people over 21 can vote. They vote for the Presidential candidate of their choice as well as for a long list of State officials.

Note 4. Electoral Vote In December the Presidential Electors chosen by each state vote for a Presidential Candidate. It is customary for them to vote for the Candidate who won most popular votes in their State in the November election. The Electoral votes are sent to Washington. They are opened and counted in front of Congress on January 6, when the winning Candidate is announced. The Presidential term of office begins on January 20. To avoid confusion the terms of office of Presidents have been dated in this book as from the Election Year (November) and not from the following January.

2 *Franklin D. Roosevelt*

3 *Harry S. Truman*

4 *The White House, Washington, D.C.*

and the Democratic Party. The Republicans were the party of the North in the American Civil War (1861–5). They opposed slavery, fought for the Union and supported the build-up of industry and big business in the late nineteenth and early twentieth centuries. Their victory in the Civil War gave them a long run of power. From Abraham Lincoln (1860–5) down to Wilson's election in 1912, President Cleveland (1884–8, 1892–6) was the only successful Democratic candidate for the Presidential election.

5, 6 *Party Symbols – The Elephant and the Donkey are the unofficial symbols of the Republican and Democratic parties, respectively. The symbols for the two major national parties were first popularized by the American political cartoonist, Thomas Nast, in the 1870's*

The Democrats fought solidly for the South in the Civil War. They were the party of the rural areas, of the farmers of the south and west. They developed a policy closely associated with reform and the people, and they became the opponents of the wealth and big business interests of the industrial north. The Democrats have enjoyed greater power in the twentieth century with outstanding Presidents such as Woodrow Wilson (1912–20), F. D. Roosevelt (1932–45), H. Truman (1945–52) and John F Kennedy (1960–3).

THE POLITICAL PARTIES

DEMOCRAT

The party of
the South in
the Civil War

Inclined to support a policy of
social reform and welfare
directed by the government

REPUBLICAN

The party of
the North in
the Civil War

Inclined to put their faith in
private enterprise, big
business and individual effort

DEMOCRAT

Vilson   F.D.Roosevelt   Truman
    Kennedy   Johnson

emocrats more successful in
th century
12-20—1932-45—1945-52—1960-67

REPUBLICAN

Harding 1920–23

Coolidge 1923–28

Hoover   1928–32

Eisenhower
1952–60

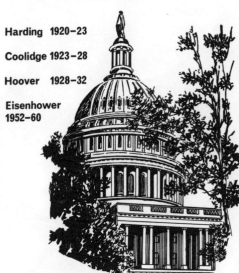

**Republicans
dominated American politics
from Lincoln (1860-64) down to 1912**

W THE PARTIES ARE ORGANISED

STATE LEVEL PRIMARY ELECTIONS

rimaries' are held inside the parties
choose candidates for the major
ctions which follow the Primary
ctions

NATIONAL LEVEL
THE NATIONAL CONVENTION

1 The National Convention meets
   every fourth year.
2 It gathers together 900 delegates
   from 50 States.
3 It elects a National Committee
   to run the party.
4 It nominates a candidate for
   the Presidential Election.
5 Each State submits its chosen
   candidate to the Convention.
6 The candidate supported by most
   states wins the party nomination.

7 *General Custer's death struggle: the Battle of Little Big Horn*

Social and Economic Change in the U.S.A.

The history of the U.S.A. from 1865 to 1900 reads more like a
television script than a history book. Sioux, Blackfeet, Cheyenne,
Comanche, Araphoe and Apache roamed the Great Plains
between Texas and the Canadian border only to be crushed
by the slaughter of the Buffalo, the bullets of the Colt revolver
and the invading hordes of miners searching for gold and silver,
of cattlemen bringing beef for the east coast towns of America
and for Europe, of settlers who stayed to farm and fence the
new lands of the West.

The construction of the great trans-continental railways—the
Union Pacific, the Central Pacific, the Southern Pacific, the
Northern Pacific and the Santa Fé—all completed in the last
thirty years of the nineteenth century, opened up the West and
filled empty lands not only with Americans but with immigrants
from all over Europe. New stars appeared on the national flag
to represent North and South Dakota, Montana, Washington,
Idaho, Wyoming, Utah, Nevada, Colorado and Nebraska, ten
states whose twenty Senators represented the farming and
mining interests of the West in Congress.

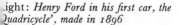
above: Early American railway – Sierra Nevada, 1870

right: Henry Ford in his first car, the 'Quadricycle', made in 1896

The railways were also behind the great development of industry in America in the thirty years following the end of the Civil War. Chicago, Cleveland, Milwaukee and Pittsburgh in the north, with Birmingham, Alabama, in the south, rose up as the great centres of the iron and steel industry. The giants of industry, finance and big business, their fortunes in many cases built up from humble beginnings, Carnegie in steel, Rockefeller in oil, Ford in motor cars, John Pierpont Morgan in banking and finance, these men became the heroes of the U.S.A. Big business in the large corporation or trust became the normal pattern of American industry.

The U.S.A. became a vastly wealthier country by 1900, but her new prosperity was patchy. The great wealth tended to stick to small powerful groups of people. America had its industrial slums, its problems of unemployment and monotonous mechanical work. Strikes and labour disputes marked the beginning of the struggle between labour and capital, and in 1912 the people turned their backs on big business and the Republican Party. They elected Woodrow Wilson and a Democratic government which they hoped would ease the hardships and insecurity of the 'little man'.

2. Thomas Woodrow Wilson, 1856–1924

The Election of 1912

Woodrow Wilson won the Presidential election of 1912. He was
a member of the Democratic party with a strong passion for
peace and justice. He had made his name as a University
lecturer and Professor of History before he entered politics.
He became Governor of New Jersey in 1910 and won attention
as an enthusiastic reformer. The Republican party was split in
1912 between two candidates, Taft and Theodore Roosevelt.
This helped Wilson but his own vigorous campaign and his
promise of reform brought him much support. He was the
people's President and born in Virginia he was supported by
the South to a man.

*10   Woodrow Wilson – 28th
President of the U.S.A.*

THOMAS WOODROW WILSON, 1856-1924

1856 Born at Staunton, Virginia. Studied at Princeton and John Hopkins Universities.

1890 Professor of Political Science at Princeton.

1902 President of Princeton University.

1910-12 Entered politics as member of Democratic Party. Became Governor of New Jersey.

1912 Elected President of the U.S.A. He cut down the Tariff and attacked the power of the big industrial corporations.
Abroad he gave a Parliament to the Philippines and American citizenship to the Puerto Ricans but ran into trouble in Mexico.

1916 Elected President of the U.S.A. for the second time.

1917 He brought the U.S.A. into the First World War on the side of Britain and France.

1918, Jan. Wilson issued his famous 'Fourteen Points'.

1918, Oct. Power began to slip from him in the U.S.A. Both Houses of Congress went Republican.

1919-20 Attended the Peace Conference at Paris. He supported the rise of new independent nations and played a major part in the setting up of the League of Nations.

1919, Nov. The Senate refused to accept the Treaty of Versailles.

1920 The Democrats lost the Presidential Election.
America did not join the League nor sign the Treaty of Versailles.

1921 Congress declared the war with Germany to be at an end.

1924 Death of Wilson.

Wilson's Reforms at Home

The American Tariff, which placed high duties on foreign goods coming into the country, had originated during the American Civil War when the government of the Northern states needed money to fight the war. It had been kept on to protect America's young industries but by 1912 in oil, steel, coal, textiles, food-stuffs and a wide range of industries the U.S.A. could challenge all overseas competition with confidence. The Tariff was an unnecessary bonus for the businessman and it made the cost of living more expensive for the ordinary American. In 1913 Wilson cut down the duties on foodstuffs, raw materials and daily necessities of life. To get the necessary revenue to run the government he introduced income tax on higher incomes and taxed luxury goods.

Wilson's real target, however, was the American millionaire and the great industrial and financial corporations which the American business tycoons had cleverly welded together. Andrew Carnegie, a poor immigrant boy from Scotland, had built up in the U.S.A. the greatest steel business in the world. By 1900 the U.S.A. was producing as much steel as Britain and Germany combined. John D. Rockefeller, who started modestly in Cleveland in 1863, was the man behind the Standard Oil Company of Ohio. He bought out or beat down his rivals and by the eighteen-eighties he held a monopoly of the production and supply of oil in the U.S.A. John Pierpont Morgan created a banking and financial empire which through loans gave him control of railways, steel, agriculture, shipping, telegraph and telephone companies, together with a host of banks and insurance companies. These men built up the wealth of America through their ruthless efficiency but their power to employ, to dismiss, to fix prices, wages and conditions of work, to build up friends and to beat down rivals was frightening. In their wealth, power and influence they overshadowed the government itself.

In tackling these giants even the President looked like David facing up to Goliath. Wilson brought banking, credit and currency more closely under government control by setting up Federal banks which were linked up with state and private banks. He made cheaper loans available to the farmers of south and west who had for many years been paying the high interest rates demanded by the private bankers of New York. The Clayton Anti-Trust Act (1914) attacked the monopolies and price-fixing of the great corporations while Trade Unions were given a helping hand by government recognition of the right to strike.

America and her Neighbours

While the Americans were opening up their country and building up its wealth they had little time to bother with their neighbours. This was how America's traditional policy of 'Isolation' grew up. The farther one moved west in America the stronger was the support for this policy.

In the last quarter of the nineteenth century, however, with her industrialists looking for markets, America began to build up an Empire in the near by Caribbean and in the Far East. Following the Spanish–American War of 1898 the American Government took over the Philippines, Guam and the Hawaiian Islands (annexed July 1898) in the Pacific, together with Puerto Rico and Cuba in the Caribbean. American businessmen were encouraged to invest money in the new possessions and in the Latin-American Republics, while the construction of the Panama Canal (1907–14), financed and built by the U.S.A. in co-operation with the new Republic of Panama, underlined the international character of American trade and policy.

Wilson's Foreign Policy

Wilson was a great believer in peace, in human rights and in justice for all nations both great and small. He gave the Philippines their own Parliament and granted American citizenship to the Puerto Ricans. American forces were used, however, to crush a rising in Haiti in 1915 and to occupy the Dominican Republic in 1916. Disorder in Mexico provided Wilson with one of his most serious problems. In March 1916, General Pershing went into Mexico with American troops to search for Francesco Villa who had been raiding American towns on the Mexican–U.S.A. border. American troops clashed

THOMAS WOODROW WILSON, 1856-1924

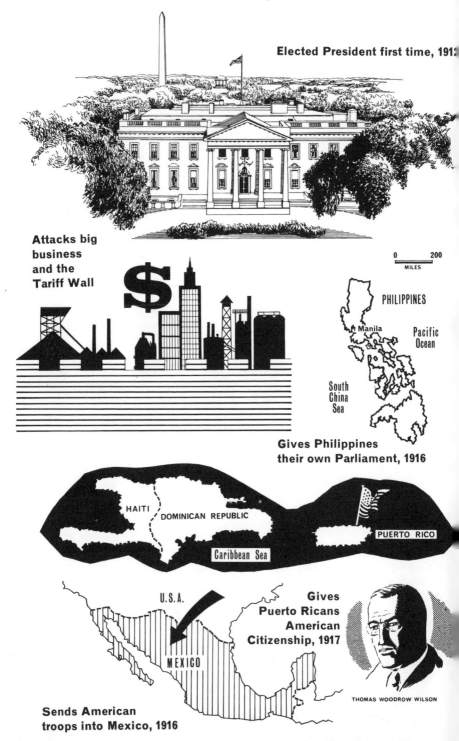

Elected President first time, 191?

Attacks big business and the Tariff Wall

PHILIPPINES

Manila

Pacific Ocean

South China Sea

0   200
MILES

Gives Philippines their own Parliament, 1916

HAITI   DOMINICAN REPUBLIC

PUERTO RICO

Caribbean Sea

U.S.A.

MEXICO

Gives Puerto Ricans American Citizenship, 1917

Sends American troops into Mexico, 1916

THOMAS WOODROW WILSON

Elected President Second Term, 1916

APRIL 1917

Declares war on Germany

Fourteen Points For Peace.

The Fourteen Points, January 1918

Attends Paris Peace Conference, 1919

The Democrats lost the Election of 1920

Treaty of Versailles

The U.S.A. did not sign the Treaty of Versailles and did not join the League of Nations

11   General Pershing

with the Mexican soldiers of President Carranza but the trouble
was patched up by a Commission of Inquiry and the U.S.A.
recognised Carranza as President of Mexico.

Wilson and the First World War

In 1916 Wilson won his second Presidential election partly on
the claim that he had kept America out of the First World War
which had started in August 1914. Ties of language and of
blood with Britain, a long friendship with France and the
brisk trade between America and the Allies which had increased
rapidly since the outbreak of war, all these factors tended to
break down isolation and to draw the U.S.A. into the conflict.
The sinking of the *Lusitania*, an unarmed passenger liner, with
the loss of over one thousand lives including one hundred and
twenty-eight Americans, shocked the U.S.A. but it was not
until Germany introduced unrestricted submarine warfare that
the U.S.A. finally came into the war on the side of the Allies in
April 1917.

The Conduct of the War

Congress gave the President special powers to take over essential industries, transport, and food supplies and to harness the
whole American economy to a vital war effort. Ships to carry
war supplies were essential, and the American Government

bought neutral ships, took over private ships, and built ships of wood, steel, fabricated materials and even of concrete.

Raw materials and foodstuffs were used with great economy so that larger quantities could be sent to Europe. Metal was saved in the manufacture of prams and toys. Travelling salesmen were allowed only two trunks and shoe soles were cut down to save leather. Changes in the manufacture of corsets saved eight thousand tons of steel a year and Americans tightened their belts with 'Wheatless Mondays' and 'Meatless Tuesdays', shark steaks and sugarless sweets.

At the Front

At sea the American Navy played an important part in the Convoy system which was introduced in August 1917, to stop the menace of submarine warfare. On land they helped to stem the last great German offensive (March–July 1918) and fought at Château-Thierry and Belleau Wood. One and three-quarter million American soldiers landed in France between March and October 1918, and they joined with British and French troops in the final Allied Offensive (July–November) which brought victory and an end to the war on November 11, 1918.

12   U.S. Marines in France during World War I

Wilson and the Peace

Wilson wanted to end war and to build a new world in which peace would not be broken. This was the aim behind his Fourteen Points which in agreement with his Allies were made public in January 1918. The Fourteen Points included a number of war aims which the Allied nations were trying to achieve and a number of peace aims which were to shape the peace settlement and the new world which the peace treaties would try to build when the war was over.

The Allies were agreed that the Germans should be driven out of France and Belgium and that they should pay compensation for the damage done to these countries. Alsace and Lorraine were to be returned to France. In making peace Wilson recommended an open, freely negotiated peace treaty, the end of economic blockades and of submarine warfare, a reduction of armaments, the peaceful settlement of colonial claims and the breaking up of the Austrian and Turkish Empires into free, independent nations. Finally as the keystone of the whole peace settlement, he advised the setting up of a League of Nations to keep the peace and to settle disputes between nations by peaceful means.

The Peace Conference at Paris, 1919–20

Wilson went in person to the Peace Conference at Paris which opened in January 1919, and with Lloyd George for Britain and Clemençeau for France he made the major decisions which decided the peace settlement. Wilson was able to fight for justice with a cool head. His country had only been slightly affected by the war. Britain and France had suffered desperately at the hands of Germany, their peoples called out for compensation, security and revenge, during the highly emotional months which followed the end of the war.

In spite of this Wilson won much of what he fought for. The old Empires were broken up and new nations like Czecho-Slovakia, Jugoslavia and a restored Poland were set up. The League of Nations, the heart of the whole settlement, was founded with high hopes with Wilson as the Chairman of the Committee which drew up the basic clauses of the Covenant or Agreement of the League.

13 *The Council of Four representing the Allies at the Peace Conference in Paris, 1919.*
Left to right: *Italian Prime Minister, Vittorio Orlando; British Prime
Minister, David Lloyd George; French Prime Minister, Georges Clemençeau
and American President, Woodrow Wilson*

Some important points Wilson could not get accepted by his
Allies. The Treaty of Versailles with Germany and the treaties
with Austria, Hungary and Turkey were neither openly agreed
nor negotiated. They were dictated treaties which the defeated
powers had to sign. The German colonies were divided among
the victor nations. It was for the time, however, a reasonable
settlement and Germany if victorious would certainly not have
offered better terms to the vanquished.

Wilson's real tragedy was that he could not get his own people
to accept the settlement which he had fought so hard to shape.
Power was already slipping from him in October 1918, when
the Republican Party won a majority in both Houses of
Congress. Once the war was over the opposition to Wilson in
America increased. In November 1919 the Senate refused to
accept the Treaty of Versailles and the League of Nations
which Wilson had made a basic part of that treaty. So both the
Treaty of Versailles and the League became the vital issues
of the Presidential election of 1920. Wilson (a sick man)

and his Democrats lost the election. America did not join the League nor did she sign the Treaty of Versailles. On August 25, 1921, Congress simply declared the war with Germany to be at an end. It was a sad conclusion to Wilson's efforts for international peace and a severe blow to the high hopes of the League of Nations.

3. The U.S.A. in the Nineteen-Twenties

The Presidents, 1920–32

The three Presidents who spanned the twelve years between Wilson and F. D. Roosevelt were all Republicans. President Harding (1920–3) came from Marion in Ohio. He was a small-town politician and newspaper editor, who was happy to follow the Republican party line of high tariffs, support for the business interests and the avoidance of commitments abroad. His period of office was marred by political scandals among government officials who were alleged to have leased or sold government property such as the Teapot Dome. oil reserve in Wyoming to private companies in return for personal payments. Harding's health broke down and he died in 1923.

Calvin Coolidge who was Vice-President under Harding, replaced him as President in 1923 and won a resounding victory in the elections of 1924, which kept him in office until 1928. He came from a farming home in New England and worked his way through college to become a small-town lawyer. Though never an outstanding man he was a popular President, perhaps due to the fact that he said little and changed less. Fondly remembered as 'Silent Cal' he was content to let American businessmen keep America prosperous, and to support them with high tariffs and tax reductions.

Herbert C. Hoover who took over from Coolidge in 1928 and remained in office until 1932, had made his name as a world-famous mining engineer and had added to his reputation by his personal organisation of relief work in Belgium and Russia after the First World War. His origins were humble enough to fit the American belief in 'Rugged Individualism' since it was from a farm in Iowa that he had started out on his distinguished career.

14 *Warren Gamaliel Harding*

15 *Calvin Coolidge*

16 *Herbert Clark Hoover*

Post-War Politics—The U.S.A. and her Neighbours

Though not a member of the League of Nations, the U.S.A. sent officials to various conferences at Geneva. She made naval agreements to limit the building of warships, with Japan, Britain, France and Italy, in 1922, and with Japan and Britain in 1930. The U.S. Secretary of State, Kellogg, drew up the Kellogg Peace Pact with the French Prime Minister Briand in 1928. The pact condemned war and over sixty states signed it in all.

The Republican governments wanted peace but they were not prepared to fight for it or to take any risks which might endanger America's prosperity and comfort at home. The old policy of 'Isolation' was strong in the nineteen-twenties and 'thirties. In September 1931 Japanese forces attacked and over-ran the Chinese province of Manchuria. President Hoover refused to support Britain in recommending economic sanctions by the League of Nations against Japan, who went on to build up her attacks and to increase her aggression in China in open defiance of the League of Nations. By 1939, in spite of the naval agreements, the Japanese battle fleet in the Pacific was more powerful than the combined naval forces of Britain and the U.S.A. in the area.

War Debts and Reparations

A condition of the Armistice and of the Treaty of Versailles was that Germany should pay compensation for the war damage suffered by the Allies. The part of the Treaty which dealt with reparations included the 'War-Guilt' clause which declared Germany guilty of aggression. Payment of reparations, or com-pensation for war damage, therefore implied German accept-ance of 'War-Guilt'. The Treaty of Versailles laid down no fixed sum to be paid. This was not decided until April 1921. Germany made a first payment in August 1921, followed by further payments in goods. Early in 1923, the German Govern-ment announced that it could not continue payment. The Belgians and the French occupied the Ruhr and Germany faced financial bankruptcy.

In 1924, a committee of financial experts headed by an American, General Dawes, worked out the Dawes Plan in an effort to solve the reparations problem. It suggested that the French should leave the Ruhr which they had occupied in 1923 because Germany had continually refused to pay her debts. There was to be a two years' pause in reparation payments and Germany was granted a loan by America to help her economic recovery. In return the Germans agreed to make reparation payments on an increasing scale as prosperity returned to their country. The Plan worked well for a while but the World Trade Depression, which had spread out over Europe as well as America by 1931, made nonsense of reparation payments. Britain and France dropped their claims on Germany and stopped their own payments to the U.S.A. In the end the Americans got back something less than half of what they had loaned and the cancellation of their war debts by the Allies strengthened the American policy of Isolation and the American desire to keep out of Europe.

The Americans at Home

The post-war period was a time of striking if patchy prosperity for America. Republican governments gave the big financial and industrial interests every support. High tariffs were again introduced and the amalgamation of the big companies on the grounds of economy and efficiency, tended to bring American industry and finance once more into the hands of a small group of very wealthy and powerful people. As in Europe the older industries in America such as coal, railways and textiles were losing ground in competition with newer forms of power, transport and raw materials. Wage cuts and unemployment in these industries led to violent battles between the workers and the giant Corporations. In Tennessee in 1927, a strike in the textile industry was smashed by local vigilantes, company militia and state troops.

The American farmer was another victim of the nineteen-twenties. A glut of foodstuffs and raw materials in world markets caused the price of wheat and cotton to fall disastrously. High mortgage rates and the American tariff which shut out European manufactured goods and therefore discouraged European countries from buying American agricultural products, pushed the American farmer nearer and nearer bankruptcy.

THE U.S.A. IN THE TWENTIES

12 years of

Republican Rule

Harding   **Coolidge**   **Hoover**
1920–23   **1923–28**   **1928–32**

ISOLATIONISM

Naval Agreements

Kellogg Peace Pact

War Debts

$

BRITAIN   FRANCE   GERMANY

They hired the money, didn't they ?
(Coolidge)

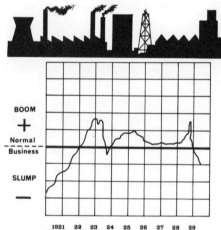

BOOM
+
Normal Business
SLUMP
–

1921 22 23 24 25 26 27 28 29

Republican prosperity, 1922-29

SALOON   BAR

CLOSED

18th Amendment JAN. 1920

CLOSED

1920—Prohibition—1933

The magic of the movies
Silent, 1915   Sound, 1927

Prohibition

Following an Act of Congress in 1919, the Eighteenth Amendment of the Constitution was passed in January 1920, which
forbade the sale and transport of intoxicating liquor. The consumption of alcoholic drinks continued but went under cover.
The 'Speakeasy' and the 'Bootlegger' flourished since a great
deal of money could be made out of the manufacture and sale
of 'illegal' alcohol. The rise of the gangster and the spread of
corruption and disorder were the most notable results of prohibition but no politician wanted to touch this thorny problem
since the country was divided between the South which was
'Immovably dry' and the North which was 'Incurably wet'.
Prohibition was repealed in 1933, and regulations for the sale
and consumption of alcohol were put under the control of
individual states.

Social Life

For many Americans the decade of the 'twenties was a period of
startling prosperity, though the new wealth tended to stick to
the rich. Over eighty-seven per cent of the people had incomes
per year of less than 2,500 dollars while only three per cent
earned more than five thousand dollars. America became a
nation of cities and by 1930, over half of her population lived
in towns, drawn in by the motor car, the radio, the press and
the 'Movies'. By 1929, there were 26 million cars on American
roads. The *Birth of a Nation* produced in 1915 by David Griffiths
was the first of the great silent films. 'Talkies' were introduced
in 1927, and by the early nineteen-thirties seventy million
Americans flocked to the cinema each week. Hollywood became
the centre of a film industry world-famous for its glamour, and
American film stars were surrounded by the same publicity
and 'ballyhoo' which now envelops the 'Pop-Singer'. Only
time and the hair styles have changed.

The cinema drew people out of their homes, the radio and,
later, television put them back in their own armchairs. The first
American broadcasting station was opened at Pittsburgh in
1920, and within ten years there were thirteen million radios
in American homes. Radio and, later, television stations were
privately owned and commercially sponsored. Business and

commerce reached out avidly to tap a market in every home and American life, clothes, homes, furnishings, behaviour and even morals tended to be shaped into a common pattern by the motor car, the cinema and the radio. Even work became drearily automatic as Charles Chaplin showed in his film *City Lights*, a bitter satire of the mechanised mass production which leaders of industry such as Henry Ford organised with perfection down to the last nut and bolt. Perhaps the words of Santayana (quoted Morison and Commager) give the 'Twenties' their best epitaph:

> 'No space for noonday rest or midnight watches
> No purest joy of breathing under heaven!
> Wretched themselves, they heap to make them happy
> Many possessions.'

BOOM AND DEPRESSION IN THE U.S.A. 1914–1937

BOOM

NORMAL BUSINESS ACTIVITY

DEPRESSION

Per cent: 40, 30, 20, 10, 10, 20, 30, 40, Per cent 50

War Boom U.S.A. goods and Arms for Allies

Republican prosperity in the Nineteen Twenties

The false boom of 1929

Roosevelt's policy helps U.S.A. out of Depression

1933 13 million unemployed in U.S.A. F.D. Roosevelt attacks depression with "New Deal" policy

Wall Street Crash Beginning U.S.A. and World Trade Depression

End of Post War Boom Depression in U.S.A and Europe

Outbreak First World War – Trade Upset

1914 15 16 17 18 19 20 1921 22 23 24 25 26 27 28 1929 30 31 32 33 34 35 36 37

4. The End of an Era—Crisis and Depression 1929–32

Financial Boom, 1928–9

The end of the glittering prosperity of the "Twenties' came with a suddenness that was unbelievable. The American Stock Exchange on Wall Street acts as a thermometer for the economic health of the nation. When prices of stocks and shares are high this usually reflects confidence in business and industry and a healthy expanding economy. When President Hoover was elected in 1928 there was a boom on the Stock Exchange and the prices of stocks and shares continued to rise feverishly until the early weeks of October 1929. This was not, as things turned out, the sign of a healthy economy, but the result of people speculating on the short term rise in stock prices, a rise not backed in many cases by any real industrial expansion.

Economic Weakness

Foreign trade had declined markedly and on the home front the depression in agriculture limited the farmer's purchasing power, which in turn lessened the demand for industrial and manufactured goods. Older industries like coal, textiles and railways which had not shared in the general prosperity, were becoming a drag on the economy. Wages had not risen at the same rate as profits and there was no solid purchasing power to keep industry and manufacture active. Much of the apparent prosperity was based on easy credit and instalment buying and public and private debts were mounting. When a lack of confidence hit America in October 1929, prices on the Stock Exchange crashed and the whole economy fell like a pack of cards.

Financial and Economic Crash

With the collapse of stock and share prices investors lost their savings, firms went into bankruptcy, factories cut production,

THE WORLD TRADE DEPRESSION, 1929-36

The U.S.A.

Oct. 1929, Financial Crash.
Collapse of Industry and Agriculture.
Unemployment reaches 13 million in 1933.
Fall of Hoover and the Republicans.
1932, F. D. Roosevelt wins the Presidential
election of 1932 and begins
his 'New Deal' programme.

EUROPE

Britain

1931, Fall of Labour Government.
Unemployment around three
million.
Formation of National Government under Macdonald.

Germany

Economic depression causes fall
of Bruening's government. Rise
of Hitler and the National
Socialist party. Hitler becomes
Chancellor of Germany, 1933.

Italy

Mussolini in control. Parliamentary government overthrown.

France

1932-33, Unemployment passes
the million mark. Industry and
agriculture depressed.
French government divided
and weak.

ASIA

Japan

Largely dependent on foreign
trade, Japan was seriously
affected. Blow to textile industry,
especially silk. U.S.A. and Britain
her best customers. Decline of
Liberal party and rise of military
leaders. Depression led to
more extreme policy, aggressive,
military imperialism. Attack on
China, 1931.

China

Setback for Chiang Kai-shek's
efforts to reunite and rebuild
China. Japanese invasion
weakened Chiang but
strengthened Mao-Tse-tung
and Communism.

India

Economic depression stirred up
nationalist activity against
Britain. Gandhi led a revolt
against the Salt Tax and civil
disobedience spread, 1930-31.

The Results of the Depression

The fragile prosperity built up between 1924-29 was destroyed.
International trade shrunk disastrously.
Economic nationalism replaced international co-operation.
Parliamentary democracy was discredited.
Military dictatorships in Germany, Italy and Japan grew
stronger.
International peace, law and order were threatened.
The authority of the League of Nations declined.
Communism and Fascism gained greater support.

workers were dismissed and wages and salaries were slashed. Farmers unable to meet their mortgage payments were sold up and the value of property and the revenue from taxes dropped. Over five thousand banks closed between 1929 and 1932. Unemployment reached three million by 1930 and soared to thirteen million by 1933.

Social Results

The social effects of the depression were disastrous. 'Pennsylvania coal miners froze amidst mountains of coal, while their children lived on weeds and dandelions.' Two million vagrants took to the roads, many of them boys and girls. 'With no money left for rent, unemployed men and their entire families began to build shacks where they could find unoccupied land. Along the railway embankment, beside the garbage incinerator in the city dumps, there appeared towns of tar, paper and tin, old packing boxes and old car bodies. . . . Symbols of the new era these communities quickly received their sardonic name: 'Hoovervilles' (Morison and Commager).

The Fall of Hoover and the Republicans

The Hoover administration could not believe that the nation could topple so suddenly from the peak of prosperity to the depths of depression. Regarding the collapse as a temporary lack of confidence they urged employers to keep on their workers. They recommended a modest programme of public works and government aid for the farmers. In 1932, the Reconstruction Finance Corporation was set up to lend money to railways, banks, farming, industry and commerce, but this measure was taken rather reluctantly and relief was slow in even trickling down to the people.

The collapse of 1929 brought an end to the Republican philosophy of rugged individualism and to the era of unrestricted business enterprise. Big business was shown to have feet of clay. Both Hoover's government of efficiency experts and the business, financial and industrial leaders whom they supported, were as baffled by the problems of depression as were the ordinary people. In the 1932 election America turned to the Democrats and to F. D. Roosevelt to get themselves out of their troubles.

THE DEPRESSION, 1929-33

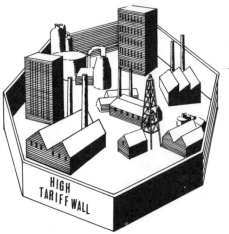

High Tariff shuts out foreign trade

Agricultural depression

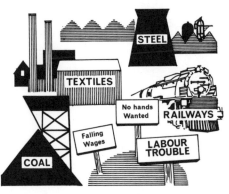

Older industries in decline.
Drag on national economy

The Wall Street crash

Unemployed 13 million in 1933

1932 Election

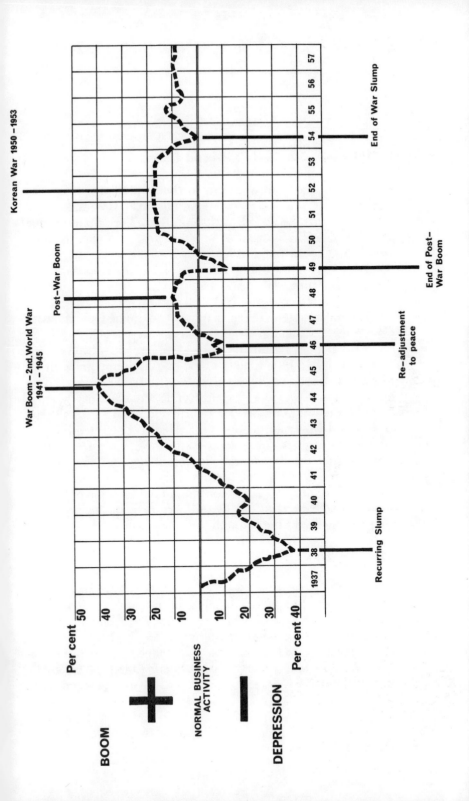

5.   F. D. Roosevelt and the New Deal, 1932–6

F. D. Roosevelt—Early Life and Career

Franklin D. Roosevelt was born in 1882 and died in 1945. He was educated at Harvard University and Columbia Law School. In 1910 he was elected to the New York State Senate, and served as State Senator for three years. In spite of their wealth and social position his branch of the family supported the Democratic party and Roosevelt stood behind Wilson in the 1912 election. He worked in Wilson's administration as Assistant Secretary of the Navy after the Democrats won the Presidential election. In 1920 he was nominated to run with Cox in the Presidential election, but the Republicans won and drove the Democrats into the political wilderness for twelve years.

Roosevelt had little time to brood on this disappointment for he was struck down by paralysis and needed seven years to fight his way back to health, though he remained partly paralysed for the rest of his life. He returned to politics in 1928, and was elected Governor of New York. He was re-elected in 1930, with a very large majority and became the obvious Democratic candidate for the Presidential election of 1932.

America was hitting the bottom of the depression which had struck the country in 1929. Roosevelt, in the tradition of Wilson, promised a 'New Deal' to the ordinary man in the street and swept Hoover and the Republicans out of office.

The New Deal

Roosevelt's New Deal was a programme of government measures aimed to pull the whole country out of the depression and at the same time to reform the social and economic organisation of America. Most of the ideas had been tried before: government control of business and finance, social justice for the individual and conservation of America's natural resources, but the New Deal was exceptional because as a programme of

F. D. ROOSEVELT'S NEW DEAL,

1933-35

National Recovery Act, 1933
1 Speed up industrial production
2 Spread employment
3 Raise wages, cut hours
4 4 million workers taken back
   in one year

Agricultural Adjustments Act, 1933
1 Crop acreage cut, to push up
   prices
2 Government compensation
3 Cheaper loans for
   farmers

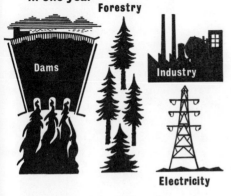 

Tennessee Valley Authority, 1933
1 Dams built
2 New forests planted, river cleared
3 Farmers settled on better land

Public Works—Employment
State governments helped
to build schools, houses,
roads, etc. to provide
more jobs, 1933-35

Money and Banking, 1933
1 Paper Currency
2 Low interest rates
3 Cheap loans to industry
   and farmers

Federal Social Security Board, 1935
1 Partnership between Federal
   government and local State governments
2 Old age pensions, unemployment
   insurance, public health schemes

reform it went much deeper and much faster than anything which had preceded it. The breakdown of business and finance and the social hardships caused by the depression gave Roosevelt and his administration an authority and power which few previous governments had ever wielded.

The Programme of Reform-Banking and Finance

In April 1933 America went off the Gold Standard and on to a managed paper currency which by lowering the value of money pushed up prices. The government pumped money and credit into the economy by lowering interest rates and by making loans easily available to business, farming, industry and local government. Bankers were no longer allowed to speculate with their customers' money and were forced to insure their deposits with a Federal Deposit Insurance Organisation. Shares in new companies which had often no real chance of success had been freely sold on the Stock Exchange. People who were foolishly attracted by the high rates of interest which these companies promised but never paid, lost their savings when the true facts leaked out and the companies went bankrupt. This kind of fraud was stopped by a Securities Act of 1933, which laid down that full and accurate information must be given with regard to new companies formed and new shares offered on the Stock Exchange.

Farm Relief

It was the plight of the farmers which had started off the crash in 1929, and their situation in 1932 was even worse. The Agricultural Adjustments Act was passed in May 1933 to raise agricultural prices by cutting the amount of crops grown and to ease the farmer's burden by granting him cheaper and easier loans. In return for compensation payments from the government, the farmers agreed to plant less wheat, corn, cotton, rice and tobacco, to raise fewer pigs and to produce less milk. Prices gradually rose to give the farmer a reasonable working income. Farmers were moved to more fertile land and efforts were made by the government to recapture foreign markets for the farmer by making special trade agreements based on tariff reductions with nations who would give the U.S.A. similar concessions. Treaties of this kind dealing with agricultural products and raw materials were made with Cuba, Canada, France and Russia.

Industry under the New Deal

The National Recovery Act (N.R.A.), passed in June 1933, aimed to speed up industrial production, to spread employment, to reduce hours, to raise wages, and to provide money for a system of public works and emergency relief. It also planned to protect the worker by introducing regulations to cover collective bargaining and trade union organisation.

The Act fixed working hours for industrial workers at 36 per week and at 40 for clerical workers. A minimum wage of 40 cents per hour was laid down. Over 23 million workers benefited from the new regulations and within a year 4 million unemployed were taken back into industry.

As the general situation improved, the N.R.A. came in for heavy criticism and in 1935 it was declared unconstitutional by the Supreme Court. Large Corporations often sidestepped the regulations and the small firm felt it was put at a disadvantage. Consumers were annoyed at the cost of the scheme and the workers themselves were disappointed with its results. It was, however, a comprehensive, courageous and effective step towards recovery and social reform.

Labour and the New Deal

Apart from the regulations regarding wages and working hours already mentioned, the N.R.A. guaranteed to the worker the right to form Trade Unions and to engage in collective bargaining. It set up in 1937 a National Labour Relations Board to investigate any move by employers to interfere in Trade Union activities or to stop the normal process of collective bargaining and the Committee of Industrial Organisations (C.I.O.) under the leadership of John L. Lewis set out to organise skilled, unskilled and white collar workers on an industrial basis in contrast to the older craft unions of the American Federation of

Labour (A.F.L.). The U.S. Steel Corporation recognised the
C.I.O. in 1937, but General Motors challenged the legality of
Lewis's sit-down strikes and open warfare broke out between
strikers and non-strikers at the Republic Steel Company in
Chicago.

The Tennessee Valley Authority

One of the biggest priorities of the recovery programme was to
get people back to work. The New Deal programme of conservation of the natural resources of the U.S.A. not only provided great schemes of public works but repaired the damage
done to forests and soil by unrestrained private enterprise. In
March 1933 the Civilian Conservation Corps was formed. It
employed young men from 17 to 25 to fight forest fires, to deal
with plant and animal diseases, to stock rivers with fish and
to build dams and plant trees, in order to check the soil erosion
caused by flood and wind in areas where the cutting down or
burning down of forests had turned the great plains into bowls
of swirling dust.

Of all the schemes of conservation, the setting up of the Tennessee Valley Authority stood out as the most significant and
the most ambitious. The Tennessee Valley was an area of some
forty thousand square miles which spread over seven states.
It had been exploited, ravaged, run down and neglected. Its
people scratched a living from its worked-out soil. The government set up the T.V.A. to rebuild the Valley, to provide
employment and to create a new and better environment for
the people of the Valley.

Dams were built to control floods, to develop nitrate production and to generate cheap electrical power for local farms and
local industry. New forests were planted. Farmers were settled
on better land. The river was cleared and became a busy road
for shipping along its whole length. Industry returned to the
Valley and a healthy and vigorous society not only worked in
the new enterprises but enjoyed the artificial lakes, the parks
and the forests which turned a derelict area into a tourist centre
and a model of enterprise and social planning which the whole
world admired.

Relief and Security

During his first months in office Roosevelt and his government faced the problem of providing work for some twelve to fifteen million people. Through the Federal Emergency Relief Administration they made grants to individual states to get local employment schemes going. New roads were built. Parks were made and rivers and harbours improved. Slums were cleared and new schools were built. Kansas City put up a new municipal hall, Denver a new water supply system and Washington set its workers on new university buildings. Artists, musicians and writers were engaged to write local guide books, to decorate public buildings, to tour the states in repertory companies or to provide symphony concerts.

All this effort went to provide work for those who could be employed. The aged and the sick, difficult to employ in normal times, were an even greater problem in this time of emergency. In 1935 the government introduced a widespread scheme of relief including pensions for the needy and the aged, unemployment insurance and grants to encourage public health schemes. The principle behind the relief grants was one of co-operation between the central government and the individual states. In the case of relief for the aged, the government provided fifteen dollars a month per person providing the state would contribute an equal sum. Within two years every state had set up some form of pension and insurance scheme along the lines suggested by the Federal Social Security board.

The cost of the New Deal was high. The Federal government spent nearly nine thousand million dollars on relief and public works between 1934 and 1936. There was much criticism that America was going soft, that the people were being pampered. No one could really deny, however, the great work of the President and his government for recovery and reform, nor should it be forgotten that this vast programme of reform was carried out in a society which was eminently free and humane, when compared with the dictatorial régimes of Germany, Italy and Russia.

6.   Events Leading to the Second World War

'If there were one principle upon which the vast majority of the American people agreed in 1937, it was that what was happening in Europe was no concern of theirs, and that if Europe were so wicked or stupid as to get into another war, America would resolutely stay out of it.' The old traditional policy of isolation, of keeping out of Europe, of sheltering behind America's ocean barriers found new and noisy supporters. An American historian wrote, 'Never had America been so smugly complacent about herself or so sneeringly indifferent to the rest of the world' (Morison and Commager).

Roosevelt was too great a President to take such a narrow view of events but even he could not resist the strong tide of public opinion. Neutrality Acts were passed by Congress between 1935 and 1937 which forbade private loans or credits to nations involved in war and banned the direct or indirect shipment of arms or munitions to such nations. Any other kind of goods had to be paid for in cash and carried by the foreign nation in its own ships. This refusal to send arms to Europe penalised the democratic nations who had cut down their armed forces and aided the dictator countries, Germany in particular, who had been building up her armed forces from 1933, when Hitler came to power.

Roosevelt warned the nation in 1937, 'Let no one imagine that America will escape ... that this Western Hemisphere will not be attacked,' but he was denounced in some quarters as a war-monger. His personal request to Hitler and Mussolini in April 1939 to promise not to attack the small nations of Europe was ignored, and no exhortation from America could stop Hitler from attacking Poland in September 1939, the event which started the Second World War. Nothing short of a clear-cut military alliance between America, Britain and France could have stopped Hitler and Germany.

A Change in American Policy

Hitler's dramatic success in Europe in the early stages of the war (1939–41) and the growing aggression of Japan in the Far East, finally pushed the Americans into the war. The German conquest of Norway, and the Low Countries and the fall of France (1940), brought the dangers of war much closer to the U.S.A. What would happen if the British Navy fell into German hands and the U.S.A. were attacked by the Germans in the Atlantic, and by the Japanese in the Pacific?

In 1939 Britain and France were allowed to buy arms on a cash-and-carry basis but the arms were not available. In September 1940 Congress passed the first peacetime Conscription Bill in American history, and in the same month transferred fifty First World War destroyers to Britain in return for leases of military bases in the British West Indies.

Roosevelt won the Presidential Election of 1940 against the Republican candidate Wendell Wilkie. With four further years of office in front of him he was able to give more aid to Britain and her Allies. In March 1941 Congress passed the Lend Lease Act which authorised the President to sell, exchange, transfer, lease or lend any type of goods to any country whose defence was vital to the defence of the U.S.A. This Act opened up war supplies of all kinds to Britain and her Allies and was extended to Russia in June 1941, when Germany invaded that country.

In August 1941 Roosevelt met Winston Churchill in Argenta Bay, off Newfoundland. Together they drew up the Atlantic Charter which laid down for all peace-loving nations the famous four freedoms: freedom of speech and worship, freedom from fear and want.

The U.S.A. and Japan—Pearl Harbour, December 1941

The outbreak of war in Europe and the early successes of Hitler encouraged the Japanese to build up a large Empire in the Far East. In July 1941 Japan declared a protectorate over the whole of French Indo-China. Roosevelt made General MacArthur Commander-in-Chief of American forces in the Far East, and America and Britain cut off supplies of oil and rubber to Japan. General Tojo became Prime Minister of Japan and head of a

EVENTS LEADING TO SECOND WORLD WAR

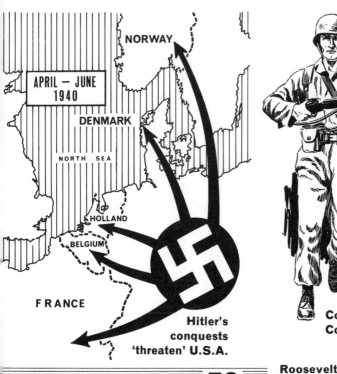

APRIL — JUNE 1940

NORWAY

DENMARK

NORTH SEA

HOLLAND

BELGIUM

FRANCE

Hitler's conquests 'threaten' U.S.A.

Congress passes Conscription Bill

50

Sept. 1940

U.S.A. sends 50 destroyers to Britain

Roosevelt elected President for Third Term

March 1941, Lend Lease steps up U.S.A. war supplies to Britain and her allies

August 1941

NEWFOUNDLAND

CANADA

Argenta Bay

ATLANTIC CHARTER
The Four Freedoms

Roosevelt and Churchill
sign the Atlantic Charter

1941, Dec. 7,
Japanese
attack on
Pearl
Harbour

Dec. 8, 1941, U.S.A. declare war on Japan
Dec. 11, 1941, Germany and Italy declare
war on U.S.A.

17 *General MacArthur*
often went ashore in
landing craft as his
forces fought and
captured Japanese-
held Pacific Islands

government dominated by military leaders. The ban on oil supplies was a serious blow to Japan's ambitions in the Far East. On December 7, 1941, the Japanese struck at Pearl Harbour, a vital American naval base in the Hawaiian Islands. Taken completely by surprise the Americans lost nearly four thousand men killed and wounded, five battleships and one hundred and fifty planes. The American Army Air Force on Manila in the Philippines was nearly wiped out by a second Japanese attack, while a third Japanese force landed on the Malay Peninsula.

On December 8, 1941, the U.S.A. declared war on Japan and three days later Germany and Italy declared war on America in accordance with the common pact between the three dictator countries.

7. The U.S.A. and the Second World War

Introduction

The American effort in the Second World War was directed into two main areas; into Europe against Germany and into the Far East against Japan. It was agreed between Britain and the U.S.A. that the European area of operations should take priority because Germany had a greater war potential than Japan, threatened to dominate the whole of Europe including Russia, and might produce at any moment some new weapon which could have devastating effects.

Britain and America achieved an unusually close co-operation and agreement in planning their combined war policy. This was due largely to the high qualities of F. D. Roosevelt, a great President in war as in peace, and to the leadership of Winston Churchill, who as Prime Minister, brought Britain through the loneliness and tribulation of early defeat into the triumph of final victory. In meetings such as those at Teheran and Cairo the two leaders met with their combined Chiefs-of-Staff, to work out their plans to break the power of Germany and Japan. After the invasion of Russia by the Germans in June 1941 Joseph Stalin, the Head of the U.S.S.R., joined the other two leaders in war talks and Chiang Kai-shek, the recognised leader of China, who made his forces available to the Allies, was consulted on plans for action against the Japanese.

The U.S.A. in Europe

In both the main theatres of war the Allies were very much on the defensive until the closing months of 1942. In Europe, the tide turned against Germany following General Montgomery's great victory at El Alamein over General Rommel and his German Afrika Korps (October 1942), and the Russian victory at Stalingrad (January 1943, see Book 2) which crushed the

49

THE U.S.A. AND THE SECOND WORLD WAR, 1941-45

Anglo-American landings Algeria and Morocco, Nov. 11, 1942

Germans and Italians drive from North Africa, May 1

The invasion of Sicily and Italy, July 1943

D-Day Landings— Normandy, June 1944

Americans cross the Rhine, March 7, 1945

Germany surrenders, May 7, 1945

Pearl Harbour
Philippines

Singapore
Malaya
Hong Kong

Dutch East
Indies

Indo China
Siam

anese conquests, 1941-42

Battles of Coral Sea and
Midway Island, May-June 1942

GUADACANAL
1942-1943

GILBERT Is.
1943

MARIANA Is.
1944

PHILIPPINES
1945

1945
OKINAWA—IWO JIMA

The
Conquest of the Islands,
1942-5

General
MacArthur
returns to
the
Philippines,
April 1945

Manila

Leyte

PHILIPPINES

Hiroshima, Aug. 6, 1945
Nagasaki, Aug. 9, 1945

Japanese
Government
surrendered,
August 14, 1945

*18 General Eisenhower and General
    Montgomery inspect American
    armoured exercise*

German Sixth Army. El Alamein gave the Americans their
cue, and on November 11, 1942, a combined Anglo-American
force under General Eisenhower landed in Algeria and Morocco.
By May 1943 General Montgomery and his British Eighth
Army had driven the Germans and Italians back along the
North African coast to Tunis, while the Anglo-American force
had reached Bizerte. Two hundred and seventy-five thousand
Germans surrendered at Cape Bon and the German Army was
cleared out of North Africa.

The Invasion of Sicily and Italy

In July 1943 the American Seventh Army and the British Eighth
Army invaded Sicily, Mussolini was overthrown in Italy but
negotiations for peace with the Allies dragged out and the
Germans had time to rush troops into Italy which in effect
became a German-occupied country.

Sicily was conquered by August, and the British Eighth Army
moved into Italy across the Straits of Messina (September 3,
1943), while a combined Anglo-American force under the
American General Mark Clark, landed on the beaches of
Naples (September 9, 1943). The Germans were driven out of

Naples (October 1943), but bad weather, the mountainous nature of the country and stubborn German resistance behind well-built defence lines, brought the Allied advance to a standstill.

In January 1944 Allied forces were landed at Anzio to the rear of the Germans, but failed to break out of their beachhead. The British Eighth Army was held up before Monte Cassino, the anchor of the German 'Gustav' defence line. In May 1944 the Eighth Army captured Cassino and the Americans broke out of the Anzio beachhead. In June, Rome was captured, followed by Florence in mid-August.

The Second Front, June 6, 1944

Operation 'Overlord', as it was called, was the plan to land invasion forces on a forty-mile strip of beach along the Normandy coast between the Orme River and the Cotentin peninsula. General D. Eisenhower was made Supreme Commander of the Expeditionary Force.

After midnight on June 5, 1944, British and American paratroops were flown across the Channel to be dropped behind the Normandy beaches, and on the morning of June 6, an invasion fleet of 600 warships and 4,000 supporting craft carrying 176,000 men, approached the coast of France. In spite of German opposition, of bad weather and rough seas, which damaged the artificial 'Mulberry' harbours, which had been made in England and floated across the Channel, a beachhead seventy miles long and five to fifteen miles wide had been occupied by June 12.

General Montgomery and his 21st Army Group held back German armoured units around Caen, while American armies pushed deeper into Normandy, broke through into Brittany and swung round towards the Seine. By the end of July, the Battle of Normandy was over and Caen had been taken. One hundred thousand German prisoners were trapped around Falaise in the Battle of the Falaise Gap and enemy forces retreated towards Paris.

On August 15, a new American army was landed in southern France, and Toulon, Marseilles and Lyons were quickly taken. Paris was liberated by the northern armies on August 25 and General de Gaulle who led the liberation troops into the capital

'D' DAY LANDINGS, JUNE 6, 1944

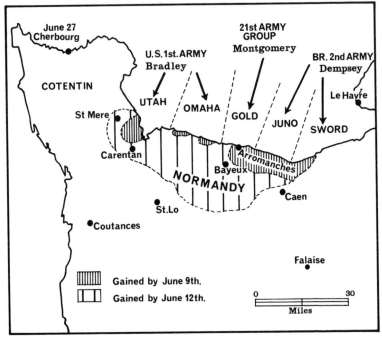

became the President of the French Provisional government. General Montgomery's British and Canadian troops pushed on into Belgium, captured Brussels and entered Antwerp on September 4. At the same time American armies had moved across France up to the German frontier which they crossed near Aachen.

Hopes that the war would be over by the end of 1944 were dashed by two setbacks. General Montgomery's plan to outflank the German Siegfried line and to invade Germany through Holland, broke down when the paratroops dropped at Arnhem to hold the river bridges, were captured by the Germans before land troops sent up to support them could make contact with them. In December 1944 the Germans counter-attacked very strongly in the Ardennes and drove a wedge through the Allied lines between General Montgomery's forces to the north and the Americans to the south. Though driven back by the first German onslaught the Americans held firm at Bastogne and

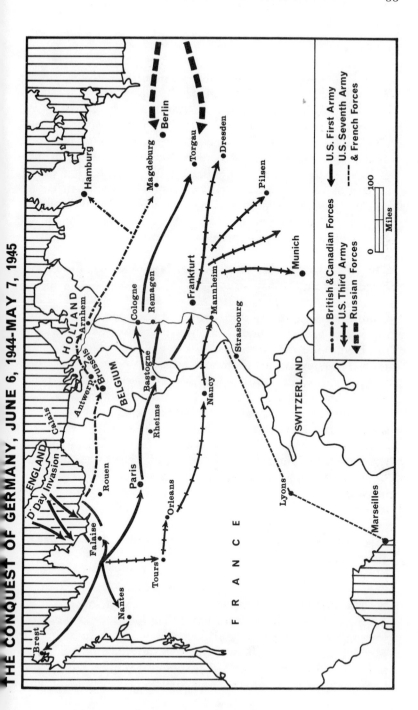

THE CONQUEST OF GERMANY, JUNE 6, 1944-MAY 7, 1945

Berlin
Magdeburg
Torgau
Dresden
Pilsen
Hamburg
Munich
Frankfurt
Mannheim
Cologne
Remagen
Strasbourg
Arnhem
HOLLAND
Brussels
Antwerp
BELGIUM
Bastogne
Nancy
Rheims
Calais
Paris
Rouen
ENGLAND
D Day Invasion
Orleans
Falaise
Tours
Nantes
FRANCE
Brest
Lyons
SWITZERLAND
Marseilles

British & Canadian Forces
U.S. First Army
U.S. Third Army
U.S. Seventh Army
& French Forces
Russian Forces

0   100
Miles

by the end of January the Germans were driven back out of France.

In March 1945 an American division crossed the Rhine followed by British units. With the Russians driving the Germans before them on the Eastern front and with Allied forces across the Rhine in strength in the West, the war was over. Only isolated though fanatical pockets of German resistance remained to be crushed. Roosevelt, Stalin and Churchill met at Yalta in the Crimea, in February 1945 and fighting came to an end in Italy on May 2. Hitler committed suicide in Berlin on April 30, and the Germans accepted unconditional surrender on May 7, 1945, when General Jodl signed the document of surrender at General Eisenhower's Headquarters at Rheims.

The War in the Far East—The Japanese Go Forward, December 1941–May 1942

From December 1941 to the summer of 1942, the Japanese won a series of victories which shattered the power of the British, the Dutch and the Americans in the Far East. The attack on Pearl Harbour crippled American Pacific forces. The British lost two great battleships, the *Prince of Wales* and the *Repulse*. Penang, Hong Kong, Manila, Singapore, Batavia, Rangoon and Mandalay fell one after the other to Japanese forces. With a large part of China in their hands, together with the control of Malaya, Burma, Siam, Indo-China, the Dutch East Indies, the American Philippines and a host of Pacific islands, the Japanese had built up an Empire which stretched west to the borders of India, south to Australia and east into the Pacific islands, as far as the Bismarck Archipelago and the Solomons.

The Battles of the Coral Sea and Midway Island, May–June 1942

For a while the Americans could do little more than hold on to the Hawaiian and Samoan Islands, keep the sea lanes open to Australia and New Zealand, and make hit and run raids on Japan from carrier-based aircraft. The desperate stand by MacArthur's forces on Bataan ended in surrender in April 1942, and the Japanese occupied Corregidor in May 1942, after heroic American resistance.

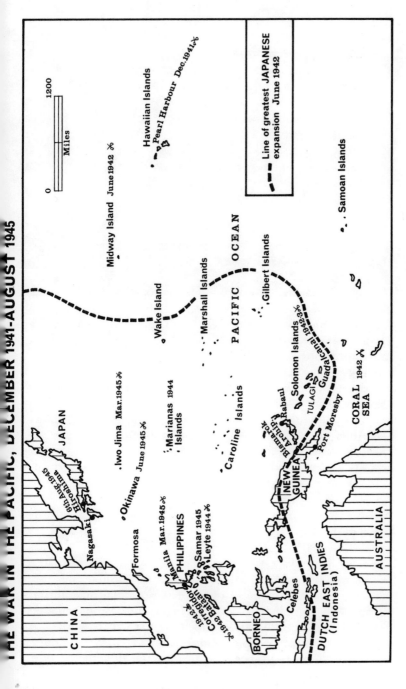

THE WAR IN THE PACIFIC, DECEMBER 1941-AUGUST 1945

19 American Marines storm Tokyo beach

In the same month, however, the U.S. Navy checked the Japanese at the Battle of the Coral Sea and prevented them from capturing Port Moresby which they planned to use as a stepping-stone to Australia. In June 1942 Admiral Yamamoto brought up strong naval forces partly to capture Midway Island but also to give battle to American naval forces, while they were still numerically inferior to the Japanese in the Pacific. The American Admiral Nimitz caught the Japanese carriers rearming and refuelling and sank four of Yamamoto's best aircraft-carriers. Midway Island was held by the Americans and as Yamamoto knew, the Japanese would never again have superior odds on their side at sea.

The Americans Hit Back—Guadalcanal

Japan lay protected behind successive island barriers in the Pacific, which were strongly defended on the ground and from the air. Japanese strength in the Bismarck Archipelago and in the Solomons was the first barrier to be broken down if the Americans were ultimately to get near enough to Japan to attack in strength. In August 1942 American forces were landed on Tulagi and Guadalcanal. Fierce and bitter fighting followed

on Guadalcanal until the Japanese finally evacuated it in
February 1943.

The Advance Towards Japan—'Leapfrogging'

The American plan in the Far East gave Admiral Nimitz the
task of clearing the Gilbert, Marshall and Caroline Islands
while MacArthur was to clear the Bismarck Archipelago. The
Americans adopted a policy of isolating and sealing off Japanese
strong-points like Rabaul by sea and air power, and occupying
and building bases on islands less strongly defended nearer to
Japan. In June 1944 the Battle of the Philippine Sea was a
serious defeat for Japanese air and naval power, and by August
1944 the Americans were bombing southern Japan from the
Mariana Islands which they now occupied.

The Battle of Leyte Gulf, October 1944

Victory in the Battle of Leyte Gulf largely due to their superior
power in the air, gave the Americans complete control of the
waters around the Philippines, and by the beginning of 1945
Leyte and Samar had been occupied by American land forces.

Iwo Jima and Okinawa

The distances covered by the military forces in the Pacific war
were enormous, and the U.S.A. needed further stepping-stones
to increase the strength of their air attack on Japan. The nearer
they approached Japan itself the more bitter became the fighting. Iwo Jima was captured after a harsh struggle in March
1945 and Okinawa towards the end of June. The U.S. Navy
meanwhile suffered heavy losses from the Japanese Kamikaze
(Divine Wind) Corps of suicide pilots who flew their machines
directly on to their targets in one final dive of death and destruction.

The Collapse of the Japanese Empire

While the Americans were pushing forward in the Pacific the
British Fourteenth Army under General Slim together with
Brigadier Wingate's Jungle fighters, had held the Japanese on

the Burma–Indian frontier, harassed them and finally, in 1945, driven them out of Burma and Malaya. MacArthur in the meanwhile was back again on the Philippines, triumphant among the ruins of Manila which the Japanese had defended house by house in March 1945. By the summer of 1945 the Japanese were virtually beaten but how many lives would be lost before the last pockets of fanatical resistance were crushed? Japan still had 5,000 planes and two million men to defend Japan itself and the many small islands they still occupied in the Pacific.

The Atomic Bomb and Hiroshima

The Allied leaders sent an ultimatum to the Japanese Government on July 26, 1945. Japan was to surrender unconditionally, accept an Allied occupation and return all conquests made since 1895. Otherwise, she was warned, she would face complete destruction. Japanese military leaders were still in favour of further resistance. The surrender terms were refused and the Americans dropped one atomic bomb on Hiroshima on August 6, 1945, and a second on Nagasaki, on August 9. The Japanese had fought a ruthless war in victory and defeat. They had sown the wind and they reaped the whirlwind. Sixty thousand people were said to have been killed in Hiroshima and thirty-six thousand in Nagasaki. The Japanese Government surrendered on August 14, 1945.

20   *Atom bomb damage at Hiroshima, Japan*

8.   The U.S.A. at Home and Abroad, 1945–60

Harry S. Truman, 1945–52

Vice-President Harry S. Truman took over as President on
April 12, 1945, on the death of President Roosevelt. He had
worked for twelve years in the state politics of Missouri and had
been a Senator for four years. He was an average small-town
American but to many people's surprise he showed himself very
capable not only of handling America's policy at home, but of
guiding the U.S.A. in her new and onerous role in international
affairs as a major world power.

From War to Peace

The U.S.A. achieved the transition from war to peace very
smoothly and full employment, high wages and high farm prices
were maintained due to the home demand for consumer goods
which had been limited during the war, and to the widespread
call for American goods which resulted from the extensive relief
programmes in Europe and Asia, sponsored by the American
Government.

Truman continued the traditional Democratic policy of reform based on his slogan of a 'Fair Deal' for all. Though he
faced serious labour troubles and strikes in the post-war years,
Trade Unions rapidly increased their membership and labour
gained a forty-hour week, paid holidays, welfare benefits and
pensions in some industries.

Civil Rights

During the Second World War the American Negro fought in
the Armed Forces, visited other countries and mixed more freely
with people of all colours and nationalities. This tended to stress
the disadvantages which he might well face in his own home
town, particularly in the American South. Separate schools for

PRESIDENT H. TRUMAN, 1945-52

Civil Rights Programme, 1948

JOBS

EDUCATION

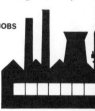

HOUSING

THE VOTE

FULL EMPLOYMENT

FORTY HOUR WEEK

HIGH FARM PRICES

Post-war prosperity.
Truman's 'Fair Deal for all'

1948 Election
Truman defeats Dewey

Post-war fear of Communism—McCarthy Trials

Elected President Second Term, 1948

The Potsdam Conference, July 1945

ATTLEE

TRUMAN

STALIN

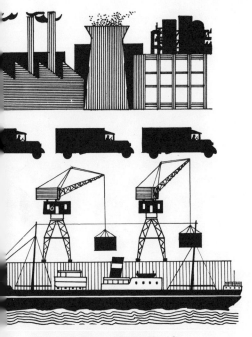

Marshall Plan—Supplies for war-hit nations, 1947-51

North Atlantic Treaty Organisation 1949

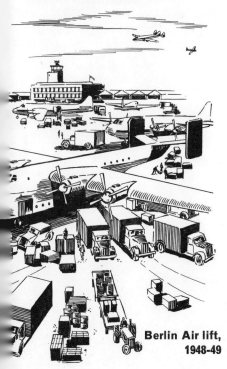

Berlin Air lift, 1948-49

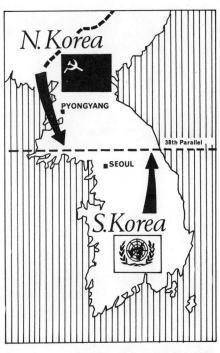

N. Korea

PYONGYANG

38th Parallel

SEOUL

S. Korea

The Korean War, 1950

his children, literacy tests for voting, together with special local laws and taxes, and discrimination against his colour when he sought employment, were all aspects of the colour problem which still existed in the areas in the U.S.A. where there was a high concentration of coloured people.

In 1946 Truman set up a Committee to inquire into the whole question of Civil Rights, and in 1948 recommended a Ten Point programme to Congress, which stressed the importance of removing discrimination in employment, of protecting the coloured person's right to vote and of doing away with poll taxes which few Negroes could afford to pay. In 1948 he fought the Presidential election for the Democrats on his Fair Deal and Civil Rights programme. Labour and Negro support gave him a handsome victory over his Republican opponent, Thomas E. Dewey.

'McCarthyism'

There was always an underlying fear of Communism in the U.S.A. dating back to before the Second World War. The final Russian triumph in the war, Soviet possession of the Atomic Bomb, the defeat of Chiang-Kai-shek and the triumph of the Communist leader Mao-Tse-tung in China in 1949, the outbreak of the Korean War (1950) and the successive triumphs of the more left-wing Democratic party in America, all these factors stirred up the fear and hatred of Communism until it became almost hysterical.

Senator McCarthy inflamed this fear of Communism by a series of highly publicised charges and trials, all directed to show that the American Government was being undermined by Communist sympathisers. In 1948 Alger Hiss, a government official who was with Roosevelt at Yalta, was sentenced to five years in prison as a Communist spy. Senator McCarthy became the most well known and the most feared man in the U.S.A.

Foreign Affairs

It was in foreign affairs that Truman stood out as a very worthy successor to the great F. D. Roosevelt. No other President 'did so much to shape our foreign policy or to set the stage on which the drama of world politics was to be played out' (Morison and Commager). At the Potsdam Conference of July 1945, Truman with Stalin and Attlee made the final arrangements which were to govern the shape of post-war Europe and Asia. His government called the Conference at San Francisco (April 1945) which laid the foundations of the United Nations Organisation and the U.S.A. saved Europe from Communism through the economic aid which poured out from the Marshall Plan from 1947 to 1951.

Truman as the President of the strongest of the democratic nations, had to bear the heaviest burden of the 'Cold War', the world-wide struggle between Democracy and Communism. He built up the North Atlantic Treaty Organisation (April 1949) as a shield for the western democratic nations. He joined with Britain in the Berlin Air-Lift (1948), and he gathered the nations of the democratic world under the banner of the United Nations Organisation to fight the Communists in Korea (1950–2) when the 'Cold War' broke out into open warfare. Master of his own government and leader of his country, he was strong enough to recall General MacArthur from Korea when the General threatened to extend the Korean war into a major conflict with China. (For further details of Truman's foreign policy, see Book 4.)

President Dwight Eisenhower, 1952–60

Dwight Eisenhower was born in Denison, Texas, of a humble family of Pennsylvanian–Dutch descent. He grew up in Abilene, Kansas, a famous cow town of the West. He chose the Army as his career and went to the American military college of West Point at the age of 21. From 1915 to 1941 he worked his way up through the Army until at the time of America's entry into the Second World War, he was Chief of the War Plans Division of the General Staff. He was recommended by General Marshall to the post of Commander of the Anglo-American force which was sent to North Africa in November 1942, and became Supreme Commander of the Allied Forces in Europe for the Second Front (July 1944). He directed the military operations in Western Europe from the landings in Normandy to the final surrender of the Germans in May 1945.

PRESIDENT EISENHOWER, 1952-60

Soldier—President, trained West Point Military Academy

Commander—Anglo-American Forces, North Africa, 1942-43

Supreme Commander Allied Forces Europe, 1944-45

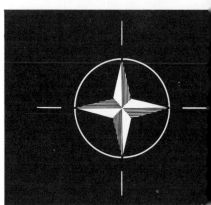

N. A. T. O.

Supreme Commander N.A.T.O. Forces, 1949-52

Won 1952 Presidential Election for Republicans—442 votes to 89

Encouraged private enterprise, business, trade and industry

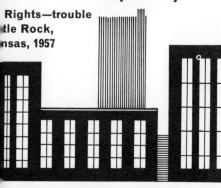

chools· White Pupils Only

**Rights—trouble
tle Rock,
nsas, 1957**

1953

The end of the Korean War

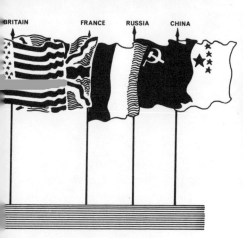

BRITAIN   FRANCE   RUSSIA   CHINA

neva Conference, July 1954,
ds War in Indo-China

0   100
MILES

Communist
China

Offshore Islands

Formosa

Chiang Kai Shek
Nationalist Chinese Forces

**Trouble over Formosa and
the Off-shore Islands, 1954-8**

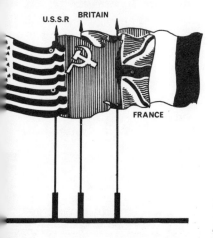

U.S.S.R   BRITAIN

FRANCE

mit Meeting—Geneva, July 1955

**Trial of Francis Powers, May 1960.
Break-up proposed Summit Meeting**

21 *Dwight Eisenhower*

After the war he remained in the Army as Chief of the General Staff until 1948. He was President of Columbia University for a brief period, but returned to military duties as Supreme Commander of the North Atlantic Treaty Organisation's forces in Europe. Obviously at home in the military background which he knew so well, he inspired loyalty in others, smoothed out personal difficulties and was an excellent mediator.

As a national and international figure he was immensely popular in America. People voted for Eisenhower, for the man, rather than for his party or for a political programme. He was never at ease in the political jungle, tended to stay in the background, to give the responsibility to his assistants like Secretary of State Dulles, and wanted the complexity of politics reduced to the military simplicity and brevity of a simple sheet of paper. In a time of severe crisis abroad he could not match as President the impassioned leadership of Wilson or Roosevelt or the professional, political shrewdness of Truman.

The 1952 Election

By 1952 the Democrats had held the President's office for twenty years. There was an inevitable cry for a change and 1952 was not a good year for Truman. The Korean war had reached stalemate, and the Communist smear against the government, broadcast by McCarthy, strengthened the call for a more right-wing Republican government. The Democrats picked Adlai Stevenson for their candidate and the Republicans chose Eisenhower, whose personality and military record brought them a handsome victory. Eisenhower carried 39 states and 442 electoral votes against 89 for his opponent.

Home Politics

The Republicans encouraged private enterprise and business interests. They removed price and rent controls. They cut down bureaucracy and were somewhat suspicious of public, government-sponsored enterprises. The U.S.A. had built its welfare state during the previous twenty years. It was now time to digest it, and conserve it, rather than to push forward into further Socialist crusades. This was the basic attitude of both Eisenhower and his administration.

Trade was encouraged by extending reciprocal trade agreements with other countries. Social benefits were broadened to cover farm workers, domestic servants and workers in government employment. Legislation was passed to end corruption in the large Trade Unions and the minimum wage was increased to one dollar per hour. Immigration laws were eased to admit more refugees into the U.S.A. and the construction of the St. Lawrence river seaway was authorised by the government. The Constitution was amended so that no future President could hold office for more than two terms.

The End of McCarthy

The Republicans had attacked the alleged Communist sympathies of the previous government and they acted on their election pledge to make the government safe from left-wing extremists. Between May 1953 and October 1954 nearly seven thousand officials who were regarded as 'security' risks were removed from their posts. Senator McCarthy was not satisfied and went on to attack the loyalty of the U.S. Army. This was too much for most Americans and in December 1954 the Senate condemned McCarthy by a vote of 67 to 22 and broke his power and influence.

Civil Rights

The problem of the Negroes in the South and in parts of the North, in New York, Philadelphia, Chicago, Washington and Detroit, continued to create difficulties for the Federal government, which came into head-on collision with the state governments in its efforts to end segregation and discrimination. In 1954 the Supreme Court denounced educational segregation and in May 1955 instructed the governments of the Southern states to open their schools to all children, white and black. Local state parliaments passed laws opposing this. They closed their public schools and enrolled their white children in private schools. Universities and High schools closed their doors to coloured students.

The climax to this quarrel came at Little Rock in Arkansas, in 1957, when Governor Faubus called out the National Guard to prevent Negro children from attending white schools. Federal troops were sent to Little Rock to keep order, but by 1961 there was not a single integrated school in South Carolina, Georgia, Alabama, Mississippi or Louisiana. The Negroes organised sit-in strikes in restaurants and on buses, together with demonstration marches and economic boycotts. Arrests on the one hand and disorder on the other made the whole problem extremely difficult.

Foreign Affairs

Few American Presidents can have had more world-wide problems to deal with than President Eisenhower. The basic American problem abroad still remained the Communist challenge, inspired by the U.S.S.R. and strengthened on a world scale by the growing power of Communist China. American policy aimed to check the spread of Communist control and influence, to unite the democratic and anti-Communist nations and to pull the neutral countries particularly in the Middle East, Africa and Asia, into the American sphere of influence. To achieve these aims the U.S.A. used lavish military and economic aid, set up Regional Pacts, gave

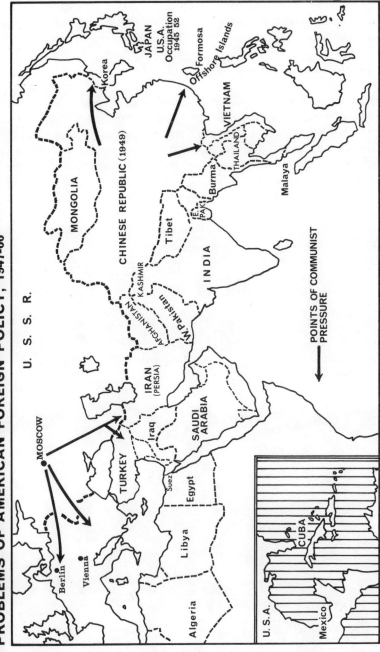

PROBLEMS OF AMERICAN FOREIGN POLICY, 1947-66

strong support to the Afro-Asian bloc in the United Nations and was prepared to employ the threat of force or force itself on a local basis.

The U.S.A. in Asia—Korea

In the summer of 1953 following the death of Stalin, and with a new President in charge at the White House, the Korean War, which had broken out in the summer of 1950, was finally brought to an end. Korea lay in ruins and the total casualties of all nations involved amounted to three million, but South Korea had been saved from Communism and the prestige of the United Nations had been strengthened. The U.S.A. had borne the heaviest burden of the war and was now committed to support the South Korean Republic and the doubtful régime of Syngman Rhee.

22   Helicopter landing supplies on the Korean Front

23 *The Korean battle continues – American G.I's 'clean up' Waegan*

Vietnam

In Vietnam the Communist Viet-Minh guerrilla forces had been waging war against the French from the period immediately after the Second World War when the French had returned to Indo-China. The U.S. Government had helped the French but the fall of the fortress of Dien Bien Phu in May 1954 made the French position in Vietnam impossible. A Conference of Foreign Ministers representing the U.S.A., Britain, France, Russia and Communist China met at Geneva (April–July 1954) and brought the struggle to an end. Vietnam was divided along the 17th Parallel into a northern and southern zone, with Communist forces dominating the North and an anti-Communist régime ruling the South.

SEATO

As Truman set up NATO to guard the West so Eisenhower's Secretary of State Dulles set up the South East Treaty Organisation to protect the East (November 1954). The Asiatic defence community included Pakistan, Thailand (Siam), the Philippines, the U.S.A., Britain, France, Australia and New Zealand. A Secretariat and defence planning group was set up at Bangkok and the ambassadors to Thailand of the nations who signed the treaty, were used as a permanent group for consultation. SEATO lacked, however, the military organisation and forces which were a vital part of NATO.

Formosa and the Off-shore Islands

The U.S.A. could not forget the disappointing loss of China to Communism in 1949, when Mao Tse-tung triumphantly set up his People's Republic of China and sent Chiang Kai-shek scurrying off to shelter in Formosa. Chiang Kai-shek had been America's ally during the Second World War and had received large quantities of American aid both during and after the war. The American Government refused to recognise Communist

24 *Chiang Kai-shek with General Fen Yu-Hsiang*

China, blocked her entry to the United Nations, and continued
to support Chiang Kai-shek who occupied Formosa (Taiwan)
and the off-shore islands of Quemoy, Matsu and Tachen.
Danger of war between China and the U.S.A. flared up in 1954
and in 1958, when the Chinese Communists bombarded the
off-shore islands on the grounds that Chiang Kai-shek, backed
up by the U.S.A., was going to use them as stepping-stones for
an invasion of the Chinese mainland. Secretary of State Dulles
declared that the U.S.A. would repel any attack on the off-shore
islands. Fortunately the Chinese called off their bombardment
and the war danger passed off.

The Middle East

With the growth of Arab nationalism and the decline of British
power in the Middle East in the years after 1945, the threat of
Russian penetration into this area became more and more
serious. Middle Eastern oil was vital to the Western democratic
nations who watched with growing concern while the poverty
of under-developed Arab states and the lack of stability caused
by ever-changing governments made this area ripe for Communist intrigue and revolution. Dulles tried to check Russian
influence by supporting the setting up of the Baghdad Pact
(1955), a mutual defence association, which included Turkey,
Iran, Iraq, Pakistan and Britain, but the curt American refusal
to finance Nasser's Aswan Dam in 1956 wiped out any advantage
which might have come from the Baghdad Pact and set the
Middle East ablaze. Nasser seized the Suez Canal. Israel
declared war on Egypt and was followed by Britain and France
who both sent forces to attack Port Said. President Eisenhower
played the role of peacemaker through the United Nations and
the fighting was stopped within a matter of weeks. Nasser
emerged triumphant. The prestige of the Western democratic
nations in the Middle East was badly damaged and Russia who
agreed to finance the Aswan Dam gained a vital foothold in
Egypt. It is only fair to allow an American historian to have the
last word on Suez, 'The peaceful settlement was a victory for
Eisenhower but a few more victories of that kind and the
Western Alliance would be in ruins.'

At the Summit

Stalin died in 1953. Khrushchev took over his post as General Secretary of the Communist Party, and by 1955 was emerging as the real ruler of Soviet Russia. Peace in Korea, and in Vietnam, the easing of tension over the off-shore islands, the Russian peace treaty with Austria in May 1955, which was better late than never, all these events brought a thaw in the Cold War, and made possible the Summit Meeting of the leaders of the U.S.A., Britain, France and the U.S.S.R. which opened at Geneva in July 1955. The big question under discussion was disarmament and the control of atomic weapons. Nothing unfortunately came of the Conference and the second attempt to call a Summit meeting in May 1960 was ruined when the Russians brought down an American U2 reconnaissance plane over Russia on May 5, 1960, and captured the pilot, Francis Powers.

Cuba

Nowhere seemed safe from the threat of Communism which left its mark on the very doorstep of the American continent. Cuba had been ruled for many years by a military dictator called Fulgencio Batista. He was overthrown by Fidel Castro, whose new régime, set up on January 1, 1959, was welcomed by the U.S.A. Castro, however, moved closer and closer to the U.S.S.R. The Russian deputy-premier Mikoyan visited Cuba in 1960, and arranged to provide military and technical aid and to buy Cuban sugar. This problem came to its climax under the next President, John F. Kennedy, when the construction of missile firing bases on Cuba by Soviet technicians brought the Cold War into the very heart of the U.S.A.

9. John F. Kennedy, 1917–63

Early Life

John F. Kennedy was born on May 29, 1917. He was educated at an exclusive preparatory school and at Harvard University. His father held the post of American Ambassador in London at the outbreak of the Second World War. The future President joined the Navy in 1941 when the Americans entered the war and was on active service for the next four years. He was elected to the House of Representatives in 1946, became a Senator in 1952, and was in the running for nomination as Vice-President of the Democratic party in 1956. In 1960 he was adopted by the Democrats as their Presidential candidate with Lyndon B. Johnson as his Vice-President.

The Election of 1960

Kennedy was opposed by Richard Nixon, the Republican candidate. The breakdown of the Summit Conference in May 1960, the cancellation of Eisenhower's trips to Japan and to the Soviet Union, the growth of Communism in Cuba and a falling off in trade in the U.S.A., which began in April 1960, all tended to weaken Nixon's chances though Kennedy's youth and his Roman Catholic religion were considered to be a serious handicap by some people. His war record, his influential background, his ability as speaker and television debater, his liberal approach to politics brought Kennedy in the end a narrow victory.

Civil Rights

Kennedy was an enthusiastic crusader for Civil Rights for the coloured population of America. During his period of office Negroes were named as ambassadors, as attorneys, and ap-

JOHN F. KENNEDY, 1960-63

1960 ELECTION

KENNEDY DEFEATS NIXON

Wins Presidential Election for the Democrats

Government Posts for NEGROES

CIVIL RIGHTS

James Meredith enters Mississippi University 1962

1963 Kennedy Round

MORE JOBS

BREAKS DOWN TARIFF WALL

Encourages trade, industry and employment

THE MOON BY 1970 ?

Gives top priority to space programme

U.N.O. BUILDING NEW YORK

Supports U.
in dealing w
'brush-fire w

Keeps the road
to Berlin open
to the West

U.S.A.

**Missile crisis on
Cuba, 1962**

CUBA

**More U.S.A. troops for the
war in Vietnam**

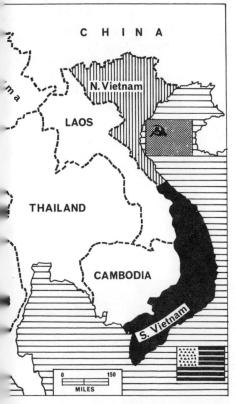

CHINA

N. Vietnam

LAOS

THAILAND

CAMBODIA

S. Vietnam

0   150
MILES

**Dallas, Texas,
Nov. 22, 1963**

The assassination of Kennedy

pointed to top Federal posts. The poll tax which prevented many Negroes from voting was abolished and by the end of 1962 a Negro could travel from one end of the U.S.A. to the other without seeing 'White' or 'Negro' signs in waiting-rooms. Efforts were made in Atlanta, Little Rock, Memphis and Dallas to open schools to both Whites and Negroes together, while in the autumn of 1962 the full force of American Federal authority, including the use of large numbers of troops, was brought into action to ensure that James Meredith, a Negro student, was able to take his place at Mississippi University.

Industry and Trade

The Kennedy administration took measures to help the distressed areas of the U.S.A. by moving industry into hard-hit districts such as Appalachia, an area of abandoned coal mines. Increased aid was given to the unemployed and efforts were made to build up training schemes for the young and to encourage them to get the most out of their education. Schemes were introduced to finance house building and to clear slum areas and industrial expansion was encouraged by generous government allowances towards the installation of new plant and machinery. By the end of 1963 there had been a sixteen per cent growth in the nation's total output under the Kennedy administration and $2\frac{3}{4}$ million more jobs had been provided. In international trade Kennedy favoured the reduction of tariffs and he passed a Bill through Congress giving him authority to cut American tariffs by fifty per cent. He brought the same approach to the commercial negotiations between the U.S.A. and Europe and his plan to expand trade by mutual tariff reduction became known as the 'Kennedy Round' (1963).

The Space Programme

President Kennedy considered the Space Programme to be a matter of top national priority and pledged his government to land a man on the moon and return him safely to earth by 1969 or 1970. New space facilities were set up in Houston, Texas, Cape Canaveral (now Cape Kennedy) and Florida.

25 *President Kennedy delivers his State of the Union address. Behind Mr. Kennedy
    are Vice-President Johnson and the Speaker of the House, John W. McCormack*

The flight into orbit of Colonel John Glenn (February 1962),
an instrument flight past Venus in the same year and the use of
a Telstar satellite to relay television programmes were the
fruits of the new priority given to the space effort.

Kennedy's Foreign Policy

Like previous American presidents in the post-war period,
Kennedy found himself faced with a host of problems around
the world, most of them linked up with the Cold War which
separated the nations of East and West, and with the ever more
powerful nuclear weapons which threatened to destroy the
world. He stated that it was his 'intention to challenge the
Soviet Union not to an arms race but to a peace race'. These
were brave words but not much more than words. Both the
U.S.A. and the Soviet Union continued to strengthen their
armaments and nuclear weapons spread to other countries in
the nineteen-sixties. The U.S.A. wanted a system of international inspection and control of all national armaments but the
American U2 flights under Eisenhower over the Soviet Union
and under Kennedy over Cuba only hardened the Soviet
attitude that inspection was only another word for espionage.
Kennedy did achieve one great success in the Test-ban treaty

of 1963, signed by the U.S.A., France and Britain, which at least halted nuclear tests above ground.

The United Nations

Though Kennedy did not regard the United Nations Organisation as a substitute for American action or policy, particularly when American security was at stake as in the case of the Cuban crisis, he did regard it as an important factor in maintaining world peace. The United Nations Secretary-General could take action to confine or cool off 'brush-fire wars' among smaller nations and in West New Guinea, in the Yemen, and in the Congo, Kennedy gave UNO every support in this kind of operation. Khrushchev's suggestion after the death of Dag Hammarskjöld in September 1961, to replace the Secretary-General by three officials, one from the West, one from the Communist nations, and one from the uncommitted nations, was opposed by Kennedy since it was clearly a challenge to American influence in UNO and was unlikely moreover to ensure the speedy, decisive action so necessary in a crisis. As Kennedy pointed out, the 'Troika', a three-horse Russian carriage whose name was given to the new suggestion, had three horses but only one driver. The Russian proposal was rejected and U Thant was elected as the new Secretary-General in 1962.

Berlin, Cuba and Vietnam

The three problems most dangerous to world peace which Kennedy faced concerned Berlin, Cuba and Vietnam. The President was determined to maintain Western rights in Berlin, and Khrushchev's proposed Russian treaty with East Germany which would end the Allied arrangements made after the war and make East Germany a sovereign state, could deprive the Western nations of any right to move across East Germany to reach Berlin. Kennedy increased American forces in Europe, stepped up economic aid to Berlin and persuaded Khrushchev that he had more to fear from a head-on crash with the U.S.A. than from the growing power of Western Germany. The treaty was postponed.

Events on Cuba led to the most serious clash of all between

America and Russia. In 1962 American reconnaissance planes brought back photographs from Cuba which showed that Russian missiles were being set up on the island. In October 1962 Kennedy placed a naval blockade around Cuba and informed the Russians that Soviet ships carrying missiles or equipment for missiles to Cuba would be turned back. The Russians agreed to remove the missiles from the island and called their ships back to Russia.

The war in Vietnam between the forces of Ho Chi Minh, the Communist and Nationalist leader of North Vietnam and the forces of South Vietnam ruled by President Ngo dinh Diem (see Book 2) proved to be the most difficult of all for America. President Kennedy wanted to stop the North Vietnamese Communists from taking over South Vietnam by military conquest, by terrorism, by guerrilla warfare, but he realised that it was up to the South Vietnamese to make the basic counter-effort against Communist terrorism. Therefore the American assistance was directed towards providing economic aid for South Vietnam, towards training their troops and providing military equipment, and towards urging on President Diem the need for social reforms. The real problem, however, was that the South Vietnamese troops were continually defeated by Ho Chi Minh's forces, that it was very difficult to introduce reforms in areas overrun by Communist terrorists and that President Diem's government was corrupt, unstable and unenthusiastic about reforms anyhow. Thus to hold off the Communist danger American troops were gradually drawn in greater numbers into the country. President Diem was assassinated in November 1963, but the governments which followed were equally ineffective in bringing stability to South Vietnam. Though America was pulled more and more deeply into the South Vietnamese war President Kennedy 'could show little gain in the situation to pass on to his successor either in the military outlook or the progress towards reform' (Sorensen).

The Nassau Pact, December 1962

In December 1962 Kennedy decided that the Skybolt missile which the British Government was expecting to buy as the result of an agreement between Macmillan and Eisenhower in

1960, was not worth producing and no alternative weapon had been agreed or decided upon. This decision was most embarrassing for the Macmillan government since there was little point in having a nuclear deterrent without the means of delivering it. The Americans patched up the matter through the Nassau pact of December 1962, by which Polaris missiles were offered for British-built submarines, but these missiles were to be placed under NATO command except in the case of extreme national emergency. When the American proposed multilateral force (MLF) which was to be manned by crews from different nations and internationally controlled, came into force, the Polaris submarines were to be handed over to the new organisation. The idea of the MLF was rejected by the French and disliked by the British. Only Germany who saw it as a possible back door to the nuclear club, gave the idea support. The Nassau agreement was confused, ill-prepared and caused much criticism. The French in particular disliked the way that the U.S.A. always kept her finger on the nuclear trigger even among

26   The Death of John F. Kennedy

her NATO allies, and De Gaulle announced his intention to set up an independent nuclear deterrent and to withdraw French forces from NATO.

The Death of Kennedy, November 22, 1963

President Kennedy was assassinated in Dallas on November 22, 1963, an event which still remains shrouded in mystery. His period of rule was tragically short but in the few years allotted to him, 'He left the nation a whole new set of basic premises— on freedom now instead of some day for the American Negro, on damping down instead of "winning" the Cold War—on the unthinkability instead of the inevitability of nuclear war' (Sorensen).

Reading

The Growth of the American Republic   *Morison and Commager*
Basic History of the U.S.A.   *C. and M. Beard*
Growth of the U.S.A.   *Nye and Morpurgo*
The Character of American History   *W. R. Brock*
Kennedy   *T. C. Sorensen*

CHAPTER I   *Work Programme*

A

1   How many colonies were founded by British settlers in North America?
2   During which years were these colonies founded?
3   When did the Americans revolt against British rule?
4   When did they obtain their independence?
5   Name the three basic parts of the American constitution.
6   Name the two chief American political parties.
7   Name any two Republican Presidents and any two Democratic Presidents.
8   Name three tribes of American Indians.
9   Write down three factors which caused the decline of the Indians.
10   Name three American Trans-Continental railways.
11   Name three American industrial leaders and state the industries they built up.
12   Name five American states from (*a*) the Eastern seaboard, (*b*) the South, (*c*) the West.

B

1   By means of sketch-maps show how the U.S.A. expanded from the Eastern seaboard to the Pacific.
2   Write an account of and draw a diagram to show the main features of the American constitution.
3   Write short notes on each of the following: Henry Ford, Andrew Carnegie, John D. Rockefeller, the Democratic Party, the Republican Party.
4   Tell the story of the life of a North American Indian.

C

1 Compare the main features of the British and American constitutions. What would you consider to be the merits and demerits of each?

2 How do you account for the remarkable economic expansion in the U.S.A. between 1870 and 1914?

3 How far were men like Carnegie, Rockefeller and Ford the products of their age or the moulders of their period?

CHAPTER 2   *Work Programme*

A

1 To which political party did Woodrow Wilson belong?
2 Which posts did he hold before he became President?
3 When was he first elected President?
4 From where did he get his main support?
5 Write down two home reforms made by Wilson.
6 Whose power was Wilson trying to cut down?
7 Name three American leaders of industry.
8 Explain what is meant by the American policy of Isolation.
9 Where did America build an Empire in the last quarter of the nineteenth century?
10 Name a famous American Canal. Which two oceans does it join? When was it built?
11 What problems in Foreign Affairs did Wilson have to tackle?
12 When was Wilson elected President for the second time?
13 When and why did the U.S.A. enter the First World War?
14 What part did American forces play (*a*) on land (*b*) at sea?
15 What important peace aims were included in Wilson's Fourteen Points?
16 Who represented America, Britain and France at the Paris Peace Conference?
17 Which of Wilson's Fourteen Points were put into practice?
18 Which of the Fourteen Points were not accepted by the Conference?
19 How did the American Government treat Wilson's peace settlement?
20 Which party won the 1920 Presidential election?

B

1   Draw a sketch-map to show the part played by American forces in France.
2   Draw a sketch-map of the Panama Canal.
3   Make a diagram or summary to show the main events in Wilson's career.
4   Write short notes on the following: the Clayton Anti-Trust Act, Wilson and Mexico, America and the First World War, the Fourteen Points, Wilson and the League of Nations.
5   Write an account of the career and work of President Wilson.
6   Explain why Wilson is remembered as a great President.

C

1   Discuss whether Wilson's academic background was a hindrance or a help to his work as President.
2   America entered the First World War too late for Europe in spite of victory. Do you agree? Was the timing right from the American point of view?
3   Discuss the merits of Wilson's Fourteen Points as the blue-print for the peace of 1919–20.
4   As a Democrat write an appreciation of Wilson's greatness.

CHAPTER 3   *Work Programme*

A

1   Name the three American Presidents for the period 1920–32.
2   To which political party did they belong?
3   Explain the American policy of 'Isolation'.
4   What was the aim of the Kellogg Pact? How did it get its name?
5   When did Japan attack Manchuria?
6   What was the basic weakness of American Foreign Policy?
7   What difficulties were caused by war debts?
8   Explain how the Dawes Plan tried to solve these problems.

9 What event caused the cancellation of the war debts?
10 Why was the Republican party considered to be the party of the leaders of business and industry?
11 Which groups in American society prospered in the nineteen-twenties?
12 Which groups suffered?
13 What did the 18th Amendment forbid?
14 Explain the terms (*a*) Speakeasy, (*b*) Bootlegger.
15 How long did Prohibition last in America?

B

1 Write short notes on: Calvin Coolidge, the Kellogg Pact, War Debts, Prohibition, the American Cinema.
2 Write an essay on Social Life in America in the nineteen-twenties.

C

1 Calvin Coolidge and Herbert Hoover were contemporary with Stanley Baldwin, Ramsay Macdonald and Joseph Stalin. What qualities would you look for in a successful national leader?
2 From the nineteen-twenties onwards Western society has become increasingly materialistic whether under Capitalism or Communism. How far is this statement true? Is materialism enough as a basis for human society?
3 Under a democratic system, a country is said to get the government it deserves. Consider this statement against the background of England and the U.S.A. in the nineteen-twenties. Is this a strength or weakness of democracy?

CHAPTER 4 *Work Programme*

A

1 When did the American boom break?
2 Give the reasons for the financial crash of 1929.
3 Give three results of the financial crash.
4 Why were the 'mountains of coal' in Pennsylvania not sold?
5 What were 'Hoovervilles'?

6   How did the crash affect President Hoover and the Republican Party?

B

Write a report for a newspaper on the state of America between 1929 and 1932.

C

1   Explain the economic factors behind the sudden financial crash in America in October 1929.
2   Mountains of coal unsold, warehouses bulging with wheat, people cold and starving. This was the condemnation of Capitalism and Private Enterprise. Do you agree? Consider (*a*) Capitalism, (*b*) Socialism, (*c*) Communism as economic and social systems in the light of their twentieth-century record.

CHAPTER 5   *Work Programme*

A

1   When was F. D. Roosevelt elected President?
2   How long did he hold the office of President?
3   What were the two basic aims of the New Deal?
4   What financial reforms did he make?
5   How did he help the farmers?
6   What did N.R.A. stand for? What did it do?
7   How was Labour helped by the New Deal?
8   Name two American Trade Unions.
9   What was the T.V.A.?
10   What did it do to restore the Tennessee Valley?
11   How did Roosevelt tackle the problem of unemployment?
12   What was done for the aged and sick?

B

1   Write an account of the New Deal showing how Roosevelt tackled the problems of the depression.
2   Write short notes on: the Presidential Election of 1932, the N.R.A., the Civilian Conservation Corps, the Tennessee Valley Authority.

C

1   Compare the way in which (*a*) the U.S.A., (*b*) Britain, (*c*) Germany reacted to the World Trade Depression of the nineteen-thirties.

2   What were (*a*) the immediate results, (*b*) the long-term results of Roosevelt's New Deal on American social and political life?

CHAPTER 6   *Work Programme*

A

1   What was the American attitude to events in Europe in the nineteen-thirties?
2   What did the Neutrality Acts of 1935 and 1937 lay down?
3   Why had the American attitude to events in Europe changed by 1940?
4   Why was the Lend Lease Act so important?
5   When was it passed?
6   Who drew up the Atlantic Charter?
7   When was it drawn up?
8   What freedoms did it guarantee?
9   Over what area did Japan declare a protectorate in July 1941?
10 Whom did Roosevelt make Commander-in-Chief in the Far East?
11 What supplies did America and Britain cut off from Japan?
12 Who became Prime Minister of Japan in October 1941?
13 What finally brought the U.S.A. into the Second World War?

B

1   Write short notes on: the Neutrality Acts, Lend Lease, the Presidential Election of 1940, Pearl Harbour.
2   Show how America gradually abandoned Isolation and finally entered the Second World War.

C

Compare the causes and events leading up to American entry into the two World Wars of the twentieth century.

CHAPTER 7   *Work Programme*

A

1 Name the two main areas into which the U.S.A. directed its war effort.
2 Which area was given priority? Why?
3 Name the American, British, Russian, Chinese war leaders.
4 When did the war turn in favour of the Allies?
5 Which two battles marked the turn of the tide?
6 When did the Allies invade (*a*) Sicily, (*b*) Italy?
7 Why did the Allied advance in Italy slow down?
8 When did the Allies capture Rome?
9 Who was Supreme Commander of the Allied forces which invaded Normandy?
10 When did Allied forces land in Normandy?
11 Name two Allied generals in Europe.
12 What caused the war to go on into 1945?
13 When did the Allies cross the Rhine?
14 When did the Germans surrender?
15 Why was the Allied situation so bad in the Far East up to the summer of 1942?
16 Name three American naval victories in the Pacific.
17 Explain the American 'leapfrogging' policy.
18 Name (*a*) an American General, (*b*) an American Admiral in the Far East.
19 Who drove the Japanese out of Malaya and Burma?
20 How and when were the Japanese finally forced to surrender?

B

1 Draw sketch-maps to illustrate:
   (*a*) The spread of the Japanese Empire between 1941 and 1942.
   (*b*) The American advance across the Pacific towards Japan.
   (*c*) The part played by British forces in the Far East.
2 Write short notes to explain the importance of the following: General Eisenhower, General Montgomery, General de Gaulle, Overlord, Mulberry Harbours, Arnhem, Bastogne.

3 Explain the importance of the following in the war with Japan: Battles of the Coral Sea and Midway Island, General MacArthur, Admiral Nimitz, Guadalcanal, Battle of Leyte Gulf, Iwo Jima and Okinawa, General Slim, Hiroshima.

4 Describe the first day of the landings in Normandy from the point of view of an Allied soldier.

5 From the films you may have seen or books you may have read, write an account of the war in the Far East, as seen by a British or American soldier.

C

1 Explain why the Allies had such little success up to 1942 (*a*) in Europe, (*b*) in the Far East.

2 Why did the Allies finally triumph in both the main theatres of the war?

3 Do you consider that the Allies were justified in dropping the atomic bomb on Hiroshima?

CHAPTER 8 *Work Programme*

A

1 Who took over the office of President on the death of Roosevelt?

2 To which party did he belong?

3 How did Truman try to help the American Negro?

4 Why was America fearful of Communism after the war?

5 Name three achievements of President Truman in foreign affairs.

6 When was Dwight Eisenhower elected President?

7 How long did he remain President?

8 To which political party did he belong?

9 Why did the Republicans win the election of 1952?

10 Name three things which the Republican government did at home.

11 When and how was McCarthy removed from power?

12 Which parts of the U.S.A. were particularly affected by the 'colour' problem?

13 What happened at Little Rock in 1957?
14 What was the main problem in foreign affairs which faced Eisenhower?
15 How did he tackle this problem?
16 Name three areas which provided difficult problems for him.
17 What do the letters SEATO stand for?
18 What was the aim of this organisation?
19 What happened at Suez in 1956?
20 How did President Eisenhower tackle the Suez crisis?
21 Why did his action endanger the Western Alliance?
22 What was the date of the first Summit meeting? Where did it take place?
23 What was the main question discussed at the Summit meeting?
24 Why was no agreement reached at the Summit meeting?
25 What postponed the second Summit meeting planned for May 1960?

B

1 Mark on an outline map: Korea, Vietnam, Pakistan, Thailand, the Philippines, Formosa.
2 On an outline map of the Middle East put in: Turkey, Iran, Iraq, Egypt, Suez Canal, Port Said, Israel.
3 Show the importance in World Affairs of: NATO, SEATO, Korea, Vietnam, the Offshore Islands, Suez, Cuba.
4 Write an account of the career and work of President Truman or President Eisenhower.

C

1 Explain the 'Colour Problem' in the U.S.A. and show what has been done to tackle it since 1945.
2 Compare Harry S. Truman as the professional politician with Dwight Eisenhower as the Soldier President. Which do you think made the more successful President?
3 What have been America's basic problems as a world power since 1945? How successful has the U.S.A. been in this relatively new role?

CHAPTER 9   *Work Programme*

A

1   To which political party did John F. Kennedy belong?
2   Which political posts did he hold before he became President?
3   When was he elected President?
4   What did he do for the Negro population of America?
5   How did he encourage industry and trade?
6   What did the U.S.A. achieve in her space programme during Kennedy's rule?
7   What were the two basic problems in foreign affairs which Kennedy was faced with?
8   What success did he achieve with regard to disarmament?
9   Give three examples of his support for the United Nations.
10 Why was Berlin a danger-spot for Kennedy?
11 How did he solve this problem?
12 What caused the Cuban crisis of 1962?
13 How was the crisis overcome?
14 Why was the war in Vietnam such a difficult problem for the U.S.A.?
15 When, where and how did President Kennedy die?

B

1   Write short notes on the following: Richard Nixon, Civil Rights, the American Space Programme, Berlin, Cuba, War in Vietnam, the Nassau Pact.
2   Write an account of the life and work of President Kennedy.
3   Draw sketch-maps to illustrate the problems which President Kennedy faced in World Affairs.

C

1   President Kennedy became an outstanding figure in America and in the World in a very short time. Explain why this happened.
2   How would you rate John F. Kennedy as President compared with F. D. Roosevelt or Woodrow Wilson?
3   Why did the Democratic Party hold such a tight grip on the Presidential office between 1932 and 1952?

RUSSIA

10. The Last of the Czars

Nicholas II (ruled 1894–1917) was the last of the Russian Czars. His abdication in 1917 closed the long rule of the Romanov royal family which had provided Czars for Russia from 1613, when the first Romanov, Michael, sat on the imperial throne. When Nicholas II became Czar in 1894, Russia was considered to be one of the three major world powers alongside Britain and the new German Empire. The Russian dominions at the beginning of the twentieth century included not only a large part of Europe from St. Petersburg in the north to the Black Sea in the south, but stretched far across Asia along the line of the Trans-Siberian railway to Vladivostock and penetrated into northern China through the province of Manchuria to Port Arthur. Russia was regarded as the natural protector of the Slav states in the Balkans, such as Serbia and Bulgaria, had an ambitious eye on Constantinople as an outlet to the Mediterranean, and was firmly entrenched in the Middle East in Persia.

Centuries of tradition had given the Czar as head of state, Commander-in-Chief of the armed forces and Father of the Greek Orthodox Church, enormous power over this huge country and its millions of peasants. The power depended very much, however, on the personal qualities of the individual Czar who was dependent on a group of personal ministers for advice and on a vast army of officials, soldiers and police to carry his decisions throughout his lands. Even in 1900 democracy had not yet reached Russia. The Czar's rule was personal, autocratic, the rule of a dictator. He had to have the strength of character, the personal leadership to enforce it, otherwise there was always the danger of his becoming the puppet of the nobles, the advisers and the generals who surrounded him.

27 *Czar Nicholas with Alexis, the heir who was never to succeed him – December, 1911*

A foreign statesman said of Nicholas II at the time of his accession, 'What is Nicholas II? Nobody knows, not even himself.' Nicholas seemed happy only in the privacy of his family. His weakness as ruler of Russia, his shyness, uncertainty and boredom with state affairs led, with a kind of Slav fatality, to the tragic summer evening in 1918, when he and his family were shot in the sordid surroundings of their Siberian prison.

Witte, Minister of Communications and Finance, architect of the 'new' Russia, builder of the Trans-Siberian Railway (1891–1905), enthusiastic developer of new Russian industry and clever negotiator of loans from France to pay for his railways and industries, had little praise for his new master, Nicholas II. Witte realised that the only way to save the Czarist régime of Russia was to rebuild the economy of this vast backward peasant state, by a policy of better communications and new industries which would bring Russia more into line with her far more progressive neighbours in Western Europe.

This effort to pull Russia into the twentieth century was not without its dangers and its problems. The foreign loans necessary to pay for Witte's plan of economic development meant higher taxes for an already overburdened peasantry. Conditions of work in the new factories were harsh and in some of the larger factories and towns like St. Petersburg the Russian workers learned for the first time how to organise themselves on a real revolutionary basis. They offered to Czarist rule a more serious threat than the outbursts of the intellectual, middle class anarchists who had punctuated the nineteenth century with sporadic risings and assassinations.

What Czarist Russia needed to survive was a period of peace when the initial hardships of an industrial revolution could be set behind her, and the benefits of the new industry could be felt in terms of lower taxation and greater prosperity. To achieve this breathing space Russia required a strong personal ruler. Overshadowed by his uncles, influenced by his mother, guided by a chance remark here and by a series of Court personalities in turn, Nicholas was incapable of making firm decisions or of following a consistent policy.

Influenced by two rabid militarists, Bezobrazov and Ploeve, he agreed 'to assert the honour of Russia in the Far East', and against the advice of most of his Ministers he sent orders for Russian troops to occupy Manchuria at the turn of the century. This led to the quarrel with Japan which ended disastrously in the Russo–Japanese War of 1904–5. Port Arthur was lost (January 1, 1905). The Battle of Mukden was a costly defeat (March 1905) and the destruction of a Russian fleet in the Straits of Tsushima in May 1905 was the final humiliation.

Military defeat was always the Achilles heel of the Russian Czar. Nicholas II not only suffered disaster abroad but also faced revolution at home in 1905. Even before the outbreak of war things had been difficult. In 1903, nearly five thousand people were said to have been imprisoned or exiled. Plehve, the Minister of the Interior, was assassinated in July, 1904, and the fall of Port Arthur led to a great demonstration in front of the Winter Palace in St. Petersburg in January 1905. The Governor-General of Moscow, uncle of the Czar, was killed by a bomb, and though the Czar promised concessions, disorders continued. The crew of the battleship *Potenkin* mutinied in June 1905, and seized the ship. In October 1905, a general strike in St. Petersburg brought the city to a standstill, and a Workers' Soviet or Council led by Trotsky took over the government of the city, bringing the revolutionary groups of Bolsheviks and Mensheviks together in one united protest. In the countryside the peasants rose up to expel the landowners from their estates.

By the October Manifesto, 1905, the Czar promised the rebels a Duma or national parliament with real legislative power and a vote for professional and working classes. The concessions broke up the unity of the revolt which was crushed in town and countryside.

The foundations of Czarist rule had been shaken but not broken. The first Duma was called in the summer of 1906, but the demands of its liberal and labour members for full control over law-making and finance were refused. The Duma was dissolved and over half its members withdrew to Finland calling on the people to rise again. The peasants and workers were not interested in questions of parliamentary or constitutional rights. The peasants wanted land. The town workers wanted improvement in their working conditions and living conditions, more say in the running of their factories.

A second Duma was called together in 1907 but lasted only a few months. The third Duma went on from 1907 to 1912 and the fourth from 1912 to 1917. Some reforms were passed. The peasants were given individual ownership of their land in place of the older system of community ownership by the village. Crown and state lands were transferred to the Peasant Land Bank for sale to peasant buyers. New lands were opened up in Siberia but the peasant in his poverty still eyed with envy the great estates of the larger landowners and continued to move to the large towns to seek work in the factories, so keeping wages low and discontent high among the town workers.

During the years between 1905 and the outbreak of the First World War in 1914, revolution rumbled underground. The government feared for the safety of the Czar unless he remained behind the high palace walls of Tsarkoe or Peterhof. They told Nicholas 'Go to Germany, Denmark or England but we beg you not to attempt any journeys into the interior of Russia. It is not safe to appear among your own people. They have had such a lot of subversive propaganda.' Nicholas did travel around Russia occasionally. There were incidents which were given no publicity but the Czar came to no harm. He was always hemmed in by police and bodyguards.

NICHOLAS II, 1894-1917—THE LAST OF THE CZARS

The Winter Palace,
St. Petersburg.
The home of the Czars

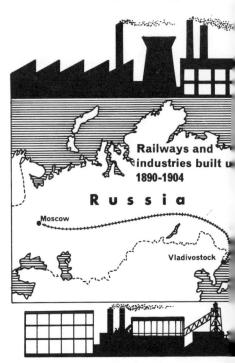

Railways and
industries built u
1890-1904

R u s s i a

Moscow

Vladivostock

Manchuria

China

Port Arthur

Korea

Japan

Russians defeated—
Russo-Japanese War, 1904-5

Parliament   Land   Votes

Revolt in St. Petersburg, 190

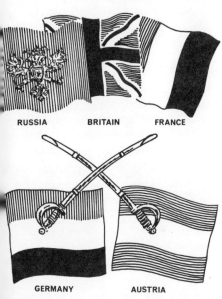

RUSSIA   BRITAIN   FRANCE

GERMANY   AUSTRIA

Russia enters First World War, August 1914

War reverses, 1917

Land for the Peasants

he War

Power for the Soviets

October' Revolution, 1917. Lenin Germans for armistice, Nov. 1917

Czar abdicates March 1917, shot with his family, July 1918

The old mystic loyalty to the Czarist tradition was not yet dead. The celebrations in 1913, which marked the three hundredth anniversary of Romanov rule, brought warm receptions from his people in the capital of St. Petersburg and in the provinces. Even a blizzard could not keep the crowds away as the Czar rode to the cathedral in St. Petersburg to open this year of celebrations. Though his time was running out Nicholas had one further moment of unity with his people. The drama of Russian mobilisation on July 30, 1914, and the declaration of war by Germany on Russia on August 1, brought people and Czar together. In a burst of patriotism the ancient name of St. Petersburg, German in form, was changed to the Russian form of Petrograd. Who would have forecast that the name would be changed again in less than four years?

The First World War started well for the Russians. They moved into East Prussia and won the battle of Gumbinnen. Their high hopes were dashed by the German victory at Tannenberg (August 25–30, 1914) but at least they had the consolation of driving the Austrians back for a distance of four hundred miles on the south of the battle front (October 1914).

The year 1915 showed rather more realistically the shape of things to come. In May of this year an Austro–German force broke through the Russian front. In August 1915, Nicholas II took over the supreme military command, signing his first order to the Army 'with a rather shaky hand', but by December 1915, the enemy had advanced three hundred miles and taken three hundred thousand prisoners. Though a Russian force under General Brusilov in 1916 smashed its way through the Austrian forces in the south, the Russians were never able to measure up to the skill and strength of the German armies.

Defeat followed defeat. Chaos grew on the railways. Shortages of food, equipment, arms and ammunition increased. Home affairs, run by the Empress with the shadow of Rasputin behind her, became more and more confused, with ministerial changes following one after the other. 'My head is bursting with all these names' wrote the Czar, but he could neither stem defeat at the front nor bring order to the governmental chaos which slowly brought the military effort of a once great army to a mutinous halt. In February 1917, now a very worried man,

28 Revolution, 1917 – the first 'Red' Guards

Nicholas wrote, 'Terrible blizzards working havoc on the railways. If trains do not start immediately troops will starve in three or four days time. This is terrible.'

On March 8, 1917, revolution broke out in Petrograd. The Czar could not find loyal troops to put down the rising and he abdicated on March 15. He returned to his palace at Tsarkoe Selo, on the outskirts of Petrograd, as mere Colonel Romanov. In August 1917, the Czar and his family were sent to Tobolsk in Siberia. While the more moderate Kerensky government lasted, funds were sent to help the Czar and his family, but once the Bolsheviks triumphed in the 'October' Revolution in 1917 funds dried up and the imperial family were dependent on alms smuggled in by the nuns from a neighbouring convent.

The final act of the drama was played out at Ipatiev House in Ekaterinburg, where the conditions for the Czar and his family became much harsher. All communication with the outside world was cut off. Meals were taken with the guards and eaten from a common bowl. There were no plates or forks. Drinking water was rationed. So it went on until July 1918, when the Czar and his family were led across the yard to a room in the basement. The head jailer brought ten soldiers into the room. They shot the prisoners,

11. The Birth of Soviet Russia, 1917–24

The Background to the Bolshevik Revolution of 1917

Two revolutions broke out in Russia in 1917, the first on March 8, and the second on November 7. The Russians, going by the old-style Russian calendar, date them towards the end of February and the end of October. They are generally known therefore as the February and October Revolutions.

Russian losses in the First World War were heavier than those of any other combatant nation. She suffered one million casualties in 1916 alone and by 1917 the strain of war and defeat had caused the cumbersome machinery of Czarist government to break down. There were severe shortages of arms, ammunition and equipment at the front and of food and fuel in the towns. Factory workers who toiled long hours for low wages, poverty-stricken peasants who drifted into the towns, and the unwilling soldiers of what had once been a great army, began to ask why Russia was fighting a war which brought few victories and little gain. Military defeat had always been the greatest danger to the rule of the Czars. Both the Crimean War (1854–6) and the Russo–Japanese War (1904–5) had shaken the authority of the Czars. The disasters of the First World War (1914–17) discredited the last of the Czars and led to his abdication and death.

The 'February' Revolution, 1917

On March 8 (February 24) the women textile workers of Petrograd came out on strike demanding food. They were joined by other workers, by students and by soldiers from the local barracks who called for the overthrow of the government. The Czar, unable to find loyal troops to put down the rising, abdicated on March 15. A new middle-class government was set up, based on the Russian Duma or Parliament with Kerensky as War Minister and later Prime Minister.

29 *Red Guards shooting from an armoured car in Petrograd*

The real power behind the 'February' revolution was that of the Workers' Soviets which were made up of representatives elected in factories and barracks. These workers' councils excluded the middle class and the aristocracy. They gradually came under the control of Lenin and Trotsky, the leaders of the Bolsheviks, or more extreme socialist party. Kerensky continued the war against Germany but only suffered further setbacks. He was opposed by the officers of the army and by the nobility. He did nothing for the peasants who began to seize the estates of the large landlords and to spread agrarian terror.

By late summer, the Bolsheviks, who had crushed a counter-revolution led by General Kornilov, began to dominate the large towns of Petrograd and Moscow and were considering plans to overthrow Kerensky's government.

The 'October' Revolution, 1917

In October 1917 the Bolshevik Central Committee in Petrograd, of which Lenin, Trotsky and Stalin were all members, voted for revolution against Kerensky. On the night of November 6–7 (October 24–5) Trotsky's Bolshevik troops occupied all strategic points in the capital without a shot being fired and captured the Winter Palace, the seat of Kerensky's government. The Bolsheviks set up their own government, a Council of People's Commissars, with Lenin as President and Trotsky as

30 Leninists besieged Duma – group of wounded Georgian officers intervened. General disorder ensued, July, 1917

Minister for Foreign Affairs. Kerensky sent General Krasnov to recapture Petrograd but the Bolsheviks drove off his forces and Kerensky went into exile.

Vladimir Ilyitch Lenin, 1870–1924

Lenin was born at Simbirsk on the Volga in 1870. His father was a local inspector of schools, his mother the daughter of a surgeon. He studied law as a young man and became interested in the writings of Karl Marx who forecast the breakdown of the capitalist system and its replacement by a society controlled by the workers, a society where the worker would receive the full reward for his labour. Through the teachings and leadership of Lenin the social and economic theories of Marx became the blueprint which the Bolshevik leaders used to build the Communist state of Soviet Russia.

Lenin was a student at St. Petersburg University and formed a workers' freedom group in the city. He was exiled to Siberia in 1897, and during the years he spent there he married one of his revolutionary friends from St. Petersburg who shared his exile. He left Russia shortly after his release from Siberia but continued to spread the ideas of Marx and lay the foundations of the Bolshevik Party from London, Switzerland, Paris and Cracow. In 1903, at a Congress in London, the Russian Social Democratic Party split into two groups, the Mensheviks or moderate Socialists and the Bolsheviks, a more tightly disciplined and more extreme group of which Lenin became the leader.

In 1917 Lenin was sent by the Germans in a sealed train across Europe from Switzerland to Petrograd. German forces had been unable to batter down the resistance of Czarist Russia so they used Lenin with great success as the Trojan horse of the twentieth century. As the accepted leader of the Bolsheviks Lenin was the inspiration behind the October Revolt. He wanted a workers' controlled state. He had little time for middle-class parliaments.

He was quick to make full use of the Bolshevik conquest of Petrograd. As President of the Council of People's Commissars and with the support of the Soviets or Workers' councils behind him, he ended the war with Germany, handed the estates of the

31   Vladimir Lenin

VLADIMIR ILYITCH LENIN, 1870-1924

London 1903

Student St. Petersburg—
disciple of Karl Marx

Russian Social Democratic Part
Conference. Lenin becomes lea
of the Bolsheviks

Lenin travels by sealed train
to Petrograd

Bolsheviks capture Winter Pala
Petrograd. 'October' Revolutio
1917

Lenin and the Bolsheviks 'rule' Russia

1 Land to the Peasants
2 Peace with Germany
3 Government by Soviets
4 Death of Czar

Lenin—President of the Council of People's Commissars, Nov. 1917-July 1918

Civil War, 1918-21— Red Russia v White Russia brings famine and destruction

in's New Economic Policy, 1921-24, aims to rebuild Russia

1924

The Legacy of Lenin

Union of Soviet Socialist Republics

landlords over to the peasants and replaced the old Czarist machinery of government by Workers' councils and Bolshevik committees. The Czar and his family were killed.

It was, however, during the bitter years of the Russian Civil War (1918–21) that the Bolsheviks leaned most heavily on the leadership of Lenin and on the military prowess of Trotsky. Landlord, noble, officer, merchant, middle class, all the groups threatened by Lenin's revolutionary social and economic programme, united under the banner of White Russia, helped by forces from England and France. The Bolshevik war effort was directed by Lenin, Trotsky and Stalin who dominated the Politbureau, a small, powerful Bolshevik committee which decided policy and saw that it was carried out. Even after the Civil War was over the Politbureau remained as the all-powerful core of Soviet government.

The dangers and harshness of the Civil War resulted in a policy of 'War Communism', in which every economic and social activity was directly controlled by the Bolshevik Government. People used commodity cards issued by the government to obtain food, housing and transport. There was no time for two points of view while the Bolsheviks were fighting for their lives as well as their ideas in the Red Army built up by Trotsky. It was during this time that the Bolshevik or Communist Party took on its disciplined, rigid character and that the Communist state emerged as a one-party state tolerating neither opposition nor deviation.

32 Leon Trotsky

33 Lenin inspecting troops in Moscow's Red Square in May, 1919

Lenin's New Economic Policy, 1921–4

The Bolsheviks won the Civil War. The foreign armies went
home and the White Russians either died as Czarist Russia died
or fled into exile. Food output, industrial production and trade
had all declined in an alarming manner, to leave Russia a
thoroughly exhausted and starving country. Lenin therefore
modified the severity of 'War Communism' and brought back
some of the features of private enterprise. Banking, credit and
the use of money for rent and wages were all restored. Retail
trade was permitted and the peasants were allowed to sell some
of their grain on the private market instead of handing it all
over to the government. The state continued, however, to
control banks, mines, forests, railways and heavy industry such
as iron and steel and engineering. It was this tight control of
the economic life of the nation even in peacetime, together with
one-party Communist rule which characterised and distinguished Soviet Russia from the other nations of Europe.

The Death of Lenin

After two years of illness resulting from the strain of revolutionary leadership and from an attempt on his life in August
1918, Lenin died in 1924. Other Russian Communist leaders

may come and go, toppled from their tall pedestals, but Lenin remains secure as the 'Father of the Bolshevik Revolution'. He inspired and directed the October Revolution. He was the head of the first Soviet Government. He gave Soviet Russia not only the theory of Marx but also the practical machinery of Communist government, the Soviets or Workers' councils, the Central Committee, the Politbureau and the tight discipline of one-party rule. It was he who won over the loyalty of the peasants, a factor which saved the Bolsheviks in the early years of the Civil War when they were in the greatest danger of being overrun.

12.   The Age of Stalin

Joseph Stalin—Early Life

Joseph Djugashvili, later famous as Joseph Stalin, was born in Gori, a town in Georgia, in 1879. Like Trotsky and Lenin he was attracted as a young man by socialist ideas. From 1901, when he lost his job as a clerk because of his part in the May Day demonstrations at Tiflis, he began to give all his time as writer, journalist and political agitator to the cause of revolutionary socialism. For long periods he went underground to escape arrest and kept on the move, travelling from Tiflis to Batum and back across Georgia to spread his socialist propaganda among the oil workers of Baku.

He soon became the recognised leader of the Bolsheviks in the Caucasian province and represented them at national conferences in Finland (1905) where he met Lenin, and in London (1907) where he met Trotsky. He became a member of the Bolshevik Central Committee and issued the first copy of the Bolshevik newspaper, *Pravda*, in 1912. It was around this time that he changed his name to Joseph Stalin—'Man of Steel'. He was betrayed by a fellow-revolutionary, arrested at a harmless musical matinée and sent to Siberia. Released in 1917 he made his way to Petrograd where he became a member of the new Central Committee set up in April 1917. He worked as a member of the Politbureau during the Civil War with Lenin, Trotsky, Kamenev and Bukharin.

From 1917 to 1922 Stalin was very much overshadowed by Lenin and Trotsky, but his appointment as General Secretary of the Communist Party in 1922, and the death of Lenin in 1924, gave him the chance to grasp not only the leadership of the Communist Party but to dominate Russia by his personal rule in a way which even the Czars had never done.

JOSEPH STALIN, 1879-1953
Part 1

U. S. S. R.

Leader of the Bolsheviks—Caucasian Province

Black Sea

Caucasus Mountains

BATUM

GEORGIA

TIFLIS

Turkey

AZERBAIJAN

Caspian Sea

BAKU

Syria

Iraq

Persia

PRAVDA

THE BOLSHEVIK NEWSPAPER

Editor—Pravda, 19

Exiled Siberia, 1912-1917

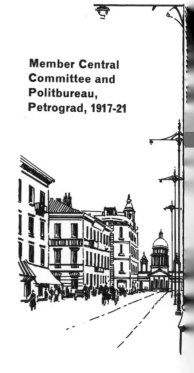

Member Central Committee and Politbureau, Petrograd, 1917-21

Stalin

SOCIALISM
AT HOME

THE CLASH
FOR THE
LEADERSHIP

1924—1929

Trotsky

WORLD
REVOLUTION

...tains key post—General Secretary
...mmunist Party, 1922

1929   5 YEAR PLANS   1939

...p the Collective Farms, 1929   Builds up Russian industry

The Clash between Stalin and Trotsky

The death of Lenin in 1924 made it necessary to elect a new leader of the Communist Party and of the Soviet state. Trotsky with his long record of revolutionary activity: Chairman of the St. Petersburg Soviet in the Revolt of 1905, head of the Revolutionary Military Committee in the October Revolution, creator of the Red Army and hero of the Civil War, was the obvious choice. The Bolsheviks were suspicious, however, of an outstanding personality like Trotsky. The party was all, the individual nothing. Perhaps Trotsky, like Napoleon, might destroy their revolution, and the policy of 'World Revolution', the spreading of revolutionary Communism to other countries which Trotsky advocated strongly, might endanger Russia by causing conflict with her neighbours. Stalin was still relatively unknown. He appeared a safer choice and his policy of concentrating on building up Communism in Russia, of strengthening the hold of the Party on the whole country, seemed much more attractive.

Between 1924 and 1929 Stalin schemed with complete ruthlessness to drive his rival from power. Trotsky was removed from his position of Commissar of the Red Army in 1925 and expelled from the Politbureau in 1926. He was pushed out of the Communist Party in 1927 and exiled from Russia in 1929. Stalin never forgot. Trotsky was assassinated in Mexico in 1940. He had poured out an endless stream of criticism of Stalin's policies from France, Norway and Mexico until he was beaten down, an old man, with an assassin's ice-pick.

Stalin—Master of Russia

By 1929 Stalin had rid himself of his most dangerous rival, but he found himself faced by agricultural and industrial problems of the most serious nature. The break-up of the large landed estates which followed the revolution of 1917 did not result in improved or more efficient methods of farming. In 1929 there was a shortage of grain and a lack of bread. The bigger farmers, the Kulaks, took advantage of this shortage to force up the price of grain and Stalin received reports of famine and discontent in the towns whose factory workers were the backbone of the Communist movement.

34 *Joseph Stalin*

Stalin decided that grain production could best be increased by basing Russian agriculture on large-scale farms, where mechanisation, scientific methods and a large labour force could be used to the fullest advantage. The individual holdings of the peasants were therefore brought together into collective farms where labour, equipment and land were declared common property and where work was carried out on a communal basis. These farms were run by a management committee supervised by the local Communist Party, and each collective farm had to deliver to the state an agreed amount of produce. In 1929 and 1930 the policy of collectivisation was carried out with complete ruthlessness. The Kulaks, the more prosperous peasants, who opposed the plan, found themselves deprived of their property, debarred from the new farms and deported to Siberia or put to work in forced labour camps.

Within ten years the collective farms produced significant results. Grain crops were thirty to forty million tons higher than under individual farming. Industry began to supply the collective farms with tractors and combine harvesters which had been well out of the reach of the peasant farmer but it must be said that much of the new machinery was badly made and spares were difficult to obtain.

JOSEPH STALIN, 1879-1953 Part 2

Hitler condemns
the Bolsheviks, 1933

Stalin joins
League of Nations, 1934

1938

Czecho–Slovakia

Munich

Stalin turns
from the West

Soviet-German Pact—
August, 1939

Germany invades Russia, June 1941

Stalingrad—Nov. 1942-Feb. 1

Russians enter Berlin, April 1945

RUSSIA   POLAND

CZECHO-SLOVAKIA   HUNGARY

Russia and her 'satellites' dominate Europe after the War

Berlin
Malaya
Korea

The Cold War—the war-time allies fall out

1949

Russia explodes atom bomb

5 Year Plans

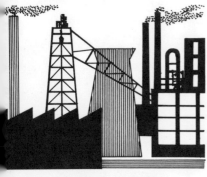

...alin introduces further Five ...ar Plans to build up Russian ...dustry and technology

1953

Siberia · Purges · Secret Police

The end of the Stalin dictatorship

Industry's Five Year Plans

The reorganisation of agriculture was essential to feed Russia. The reorganisation of industry was just as vital if Communist Russia was ever going to match the power and prosperity of the capitalist countries of Europe and America. The planning and control of industrial production by the state was a basic feature of Soviet Communism and the reshaping of Russian industry was carried out with the same determined pressure by the state that had been applied to agriculture.

Stalin's first two Five Year Plans for industry, which covered approximately the years from 1929 to 1939, achieved a remarkable expansion of industrial production. The first Five Year Plan concentrated on increasing output of coal, iron and steel. Exports were stepped up to pay for vital raw materials from abroad and home consumption was drastically reduced. Steel plants, factories producing tractors and agricultural machinery, a chemical industry, all resulted from the gigantic effort which Stalin and the Communist Party wrung from the Russian people. As Stalin himself said, this industrial revolution was not just a matter of production or economics; it was a question of survival for Russia and in particular for Communist Russia. 'We are fifty or a hundred years behind the advanced countries. We must make good this lag in ten years. Either we do it or they crush us.'

An American eye-witness working in the iron and steel industry in Magnitogorsk wrote that tens of thousands of people were enduring intense hardships to build blast furnaces, but enduring them with boundless enthusiasm. 'I would wager,' he concluded, 'that Russia's battle of ferrous metallurgy alone, involved more casualties than the battle of the Marne' (John Scott, *Behind the Urals*—quoted Deutscher). By 1939 Russia was still behind her capitalist rivals in the production of coal, iron and steel and electric power, but the gap between them had been significantly narrowed.

The Government of Soviet Russia

Communist Russia adopted the title of the Union of Soviet Socialist Republics in 1924, when a new constitution which was largely the work of Stalin, was introduced. At this time the

Union consisted of four Republics: Russia, Transcaucasia, the Ukraine and Byelorussia. By 1939 the number of Republics had been increased to eleven and by 1966 to fifteen. The word Soviet is included in the national name because Workers' councils or Soviets at local, provincial and national levels form the political framework of the state and of the Communist Party. The name Socialist is given to the republics because the national economy and the local economies are based on a national plan controlled from the centre, and on local production plans which are dovetailed into the central plan laid down from Moscow.

Russia is a difficult country to govern because of its immense size and because of its great variety in race, language and people. Thus a strong government at the centre is vital. The real executive or direct political power lay in Stalin's time in the Central Committee of the Communist Party and in the much smaller Politbureau which made the most important decisions of government and saw that they were carried out. Stalin was General Secretary of the Communist Party. He dominated the Central Committee and the Politbureau. He was head of the armed forces and of the secret police. Stalin therefore ruled Russia.

The machinery of government spread out from the Council of Commissars which was similar to a British Cabinet. Each Commissar directed one of the main departments of government. The departments which were controlled from Moscow included military affairs, foreign policy, foreign trade, national communications, overall economic planning and the political police. The Communist Party acted as an interlinking network, working through committees and organisations at all levels down to the local factory or farm in some distant Republic. It held the whole machinery of government together and used an all-watchful eye to see that everything fitted in with the master plan from Moscow.

In 1936 a new constitution put the task of law-making into the hands of a Supreme Soviet, which was divided into a popularly elected Soviet of the Union and a Council of Nationalities which represented the various Republics on a state basis. The Supreme Soviet chose the Council of Commissars of which Stalin was the Chairman. Voting for members of the Soviet of the Union was by secret ballot, each citizen having a vote,

THE TWO SIDES OF SOVIET POWER

The Government

Presidium of the Supreme Soviet
34 Members. Its Chairman is the nominal head or President of the U.S.S.R. Acts for the Supreme Soviet when the larger body is not in session. Has little real power in practice.

The Supreme Soviet
The 'Parliament' of the U.S.S.R. has two houses: the Council of the Union, popularly elected, one deputy elected for 4 years per 300,000 pop; the Council of Nationalities representing the various republics, territories, etc. 25 Deputies from each Republic of the Union. Meets twice a year. In theory the highest organ of State power, in practice too large to have real power.

The Council of Ministers
A little like a British Cabinet. It guides the work of the Chief Ministries of the Soviet Government, e.g. Defence, Foreign Affairs, Finance, Foreign Trade. The Chairman of the Council is always a top Soviet Leader and holds the title of Prime Minister. With some seven other ministers he forms the Presidium of the Council which makes the vital decisions and policies in co-operation with the Presidium of the Central Committee. Chairman 1967—Kosygin. Post previously held by Stalin and Khrushchev.

Local Government
The Union Republics have a Supreme Soviet (1 House), a Presidium and Council of Ministers. Regions, territories, cities, rural districts, have a Soviet elected for 2 years and Executive Committees to direct government in the local area.

The Communist Party

Presidium of the Central Committee
Previously known as Politbureau. 12 full members including top leaders. Works out policies and decisions for whole of U.S.S.R. Stalin, Khrushchev, Brezhnev and Kosygin have all been members in their turn.

The Secretariat
1st Secretary (Secretary-General) is a vital post. Previously held by Stalin, Khrushchev and in 1967—Brezhnev. Secretariat directs day-to-day activities of the party and meets frequently.

The Central Committee
Large Committee of 175 full members. Meets once in 6 months or oftener as required. In theory directs entire work of the Party—in practice confirms the policies and decisions of the leaders in the Presidium and Secretariat.

The Party Congress
Nearly 5,000 delegates attended 22nd Party Congress in 1961. A little like an American Party Convention. In theory the source of all power in the Party. In practice endorses decisions and policies passed down from above.

Local Party Organisation
There are local Party Committees based on Republics of the Union, regions, territories, cities, rural districts, schools, factories and farms. Below district and city level any 3 members of the Party can form a Party cell to spread propaganda and recruit new members.

though there was only one party to vote for—the Communist Party.

Stalin died in 1953, and none of his successors has wielded the same immense personal power which he built up and held over so many years. Political power in Soviet Russia still lies, however, in the hands of the Communist Party, in its Central Committee and in the Presidium of the Central Committee which has replaced the Politbureau. The supreme law-making body is still the Supreme Soviet with its Council of the Union and Council of Nationalities, while the executive work of government is carried out by the Council of Commissars, now called the Council of Ministers. It is significant, however, that since the overthrow of Khrushchev in 1964, personal power at the top has been shared between Brezhnev and Kosygin. Brezhnev became the Party leader and the leading member of the Central Committee and of its Presidium, while Kosygin became Prime Minister or Chairman of the Council of Ministers.

13. Nikita Khrushchev, 1894–

Early Life

Nikita Khrushchev was born in the village of Kalinovka, on the Ukrainian border not far from Kursk. He went to the local parish school and became the first member of his family to learn to read and write. At fifteen he went with his father to the town of Yuzovka to work in the coal pits of the Don basin and became a fitter in the pit workshops. He soon joined the Workers' Committee and was introduced to Lazar Kaganovich, the local Bolshevik organiser. He joined the Communist Party in 1918 and took part in the Russian Civil War as a junior Commissar in the Red Guards.

He returned to the pit in 1920 and was promoted to assistant manager. He became secretary of the local Communist Party and in 1929 was called to join Kaganovich in Moscow. In 1934 he became a full member of the Communist Central Committee and was given the task of looking after Moscow and the region around the city. The Moscow Underground Railway remains as a reminder of the driving energy of Khrushchev, who was responsible for its construction. He returned south in 1938 as First Secretary of the Communist Party in Kiev and served on War Councils during the Second World War. In 1944 he became Prime Minister of the Ukraine, responsible for postwar reconstruction, and returned to Moscow in 1949 to take up again his old position as the city's First Secretary as well as being responsible to the Soviet Central Committee for agricultural policy. His handling of agriculture, on which he always considered himself an expert, brought him into disgrace, but he still managed to hold on to a controlling position in the Communist Party machine, and by March 1953, when Stalin died 'all the threads of the party organisation were gathered neatly into Khrushchev's hands' (Page and Burg).

The Last Years of Stalin, 1941–53

The War Years (1941–5) strengthened Stalin's grip on Russia and he came out of the war with even more power and far greater international stature. It was Stalin who stood fast in face of the disasters which followed the first German onslaught in 1941. He stayed in Moscow on October 16, 1941, when half the population had fled in fear from the approaching Germans. He found new generals, Zhukov, Rokossovsky and Vatutin, to throw back the Germans. The Battle of Stalingrad (see Book 4) was a personal triumph for him and the final Russian victory in 1945 was utterly complete. In international diplomacy he handled Churchill and Roosevelt cleverly and at the Potsdam Conference he stood out as the central figure, the last of the great war leaders still in power.

Russia came out of the war as one of the two greatest powers in the world. Stalin gathered together an Empire of 'Satellite' states which spread from the Baltic to the Balkans, and Russian influence stretched more deeply into Western Europe than ever before. The wartime co-operation between Russia and the Western Allies turned sour after the war. The West feared the growing power of Communism while Russia felt threatened by the power and the atomic weapons of the U.S.A. In 1949 Russia exploded her own atomic bomb and relations between Russia and her previous allies, the U.S.A., Britain and France, reached crisis point when the Russians closed the roads from the West into Berlin (1948–9). Thus the 'cold war' developed between the West and Russia. Beginning in Europe it spread to Asia, into Malaya and Korea.

At home Russia made great strides in post-war reconstruction and in science and technology with the help of German scientists. Stalin introduced a fourth Five Year Plan in 1946, to restore the war-ravaged areas and to rebuild industry and agriculture. Russia stripped Austria and Eastern Germany of industrial equipment and replaced Germany as a supplier of industrial goods to Eastern Europe. The period of the 'cold war' was marked by suspicion and fear at home as well as abroad. Between 1948 and 1952 many Russians were deported to Siberia and top officials in the party and in the government were 'purged'. Beria, the head of the secret police, inspired

NIKITA KHRUSHCHEV, 1894- Part 1

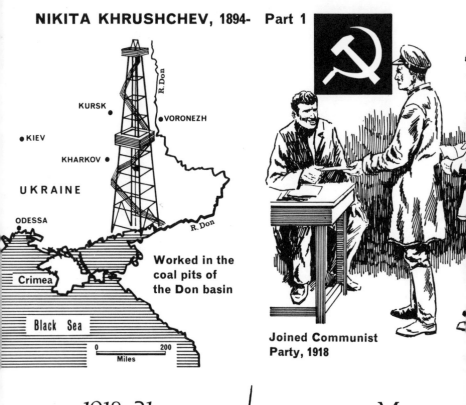

KURSK
VORONEZH
KIEV
KHARKOV
UKRAINE
ODESSA
Crimea
Black Sea
R. Don
R. Don

0   200
Miles

Worked in the
coal pits of
the Don basin

Joined Communist
Party, 1918

1918-21

Junior Commissar—Red Guards

Moscow

1934, member
Communist Pa
Central
Committe

Responsible for
city of Moscow

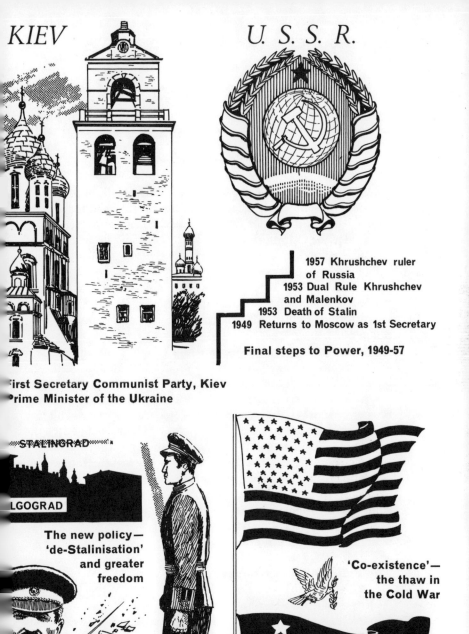

KIEV

U. S. S. R.

1957 Khrushchev ruler of Russia
1953 Dual Rule Khrushchev and Malenkov
1953 Death of Stalin
1949 Returns to Moscow as 1st Secretary

Final steps to Power, 1949-57

First Secretary Communist Party, Kiev
Prime Minister of the Ukraine

STALINGRAD

VOLGOGRAD

The new policy—
'de-Stalinisation'
and greater
freedom

'Co-existence'—
the thaw in
the Cold War

widespread fear. The long shadow of Stalin's dictatorship stretched out to the year of his death, when there were at least three to four million people in slave labour camps in Russia.

Khrushchev's Rise to Power, 1953–7

The removal of Beria a few months after the death of Stalin put the government of Russia nominally in the hands of both Malenkov as Premier of Russia and Khrushchev as Secretary-General of the Communist Party. Khrushchev was able, however, to use his position as Secretary-General to gain increasing influence over the powerful Central Committee of the Communist Party, and when the final struggle for power came in 1957, Khrushchev gained the support of the Central Committee against his rivals, Malenkov, Molotov, Kaganovich and Shepilov.

Khrushchev got rid of his rivals by giving them insignificant positions in remote places. This policy was in line with the liberalisation of Russian policy which followed Stalin's death in 1953. The power of the secret police was cut down and the Soviet citizen was given more protection against arbitrary arrest and imprisonment. A report by Khrushchev to the Twentieth Congress of the Communist Party in 1956 and a statement by the Central Committee in June of the same year, condemned the harshness of Stalin's rule and the dangers of the over-powerful personality. This rush towards freedom nearly ruined Khrushchev for it inspired the anti-Soviet rising in Hungary in 1956, which was crushed however, with all the brutality of the Stalin era.

The Policy of Khrushchev, 1957–64

As head of the Russian Government from 1957 to 1964, Khrushchev gave Soviet Russia a new public image. Stalin had been the secret man of the Kremlin, but Khrushchev became the most publicized globe-trotter. The bitter crises of Stalin's 'Cold War' always threatened to turn into a fighting war but Khrushchev emphasised the more optimistic and peaceful policy of 'co-existence' between Communism and the West. His special aim was to achieve some basic agreement with the U.S.A. and so bridge the gap which divided the worlds of East and West.

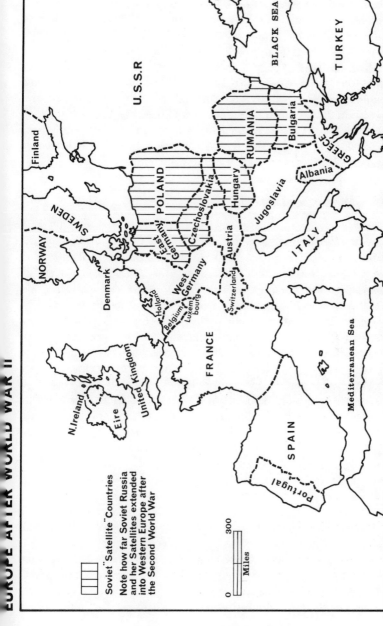

EUROPE AFTER WORLD WAR II

Soviet "Satellite" Countries

Note how far Soviet Russia and her Satellites extended into Western Europe after the Second World War

0   300

Miles

Russian interests of course remained paramount in Khrushchev's policy as they had done previously under Stalin. Khrushchev condemned Adenauer's Germany for the Russians still remembered with fear and bitterness the German invasion of their country. He posed as the champion of the independent nations in Africa and sought to win the uncommitted nations such as India, Egypt and Indonesia over to the Russian camp. He condemned colonialism and the efforts of the West to bring stability to South-East Asia through SEATO. He wooed the world on his visits to England, the U.S.A., India, Burma and Afghanistan, but his courtship was based on the economic and technological progress of Russia. It was a straight challenge of peaceful competition with the capitalist world.

Khrushchev and the U.S.A.

Khrushchev's visit to the U.S.A. in 1959 was the crowning achievement of his career. In Russian eyes he was the fighter for peace and disarmament, the man who had spoken on equal terms with the President of the U.S.A., who had made friends with peace-loving Americans and shown that peaceful co-existence and peaceful competition were not only practical but were in fact the basic solution to the world's problems. The films of the visit which were widely shown in Russia underlined the drama of the 'barefooted miner boy climbing the steps of the White House'.

On May 5, 1960, Khrushchev announced in a speech to the Supreme Soviet that an American U2 reconnaissance plane had been shot down over Russian territory and that the American pilot, Francis Powers, was in Russian hands. The Russians demanded an apology and an end to the U2 flights. Relations between Khrushchev and President Eisenhower became very strained and the proposed Summit Meeting between Russia, the U.S.A., Britain and France was indefinitely postponed.

Relations between East and West grew less and less cordial and when Khrushchev went to New York in September 1960, to attend a meeting of the General Assembly with other heads of State, it was a truculent, defiant, table-banging Khrushchev who caught the eye of world publicity. He set out to court the African leaders, to emphasise his friendship with Fidel Castro of

35 *Nikita Khrushchev addresses the 15th session of the United Nations General Assembly in October, 1960*

Cuba and to challenge the United Nations Organisation and in particular the Secretary-General, Dag Hammarskjöld, as the tool of the American Government.

During 1961 tension continued to grow between the American and Soviet governments. In April 1961 the Russians sent the first man, Yuri Gagarin, into orbit in space. This brought great prestige to Soviet Russia and shocked the Americans. In the same month the American-supported invasion of Cuba was crushed by Castro at the Bay of Pigs, and Russia and Cuba moved closer together. In June 1961 the Russian Government threatened to sign a separate peace treaty with East Germany which would deny access to Berlin to the Western powers, and in August the Russians closed off East Berlin by building the Berlin Wall. In September 1961 Dag Hammarskjöld was killed in an air crash in the Congo. Khrushchev put forward his suggestion for three officials to replace the Secretary-General, one to represent the Soviet bloc, one to represent the West, and one to be chosen by the neutral powers. The Russians hoped to get the support of two out of the three officials. The 'Troika' suggestion was turned down and U Thant succeeded Dag Hammarskjöld as Secretary-General of UNO in 1962.

NIKITA KHRUSHCHEV, 1894-   Part 2

Khrushchev visits
New York, 1959

Summit Meeting
cancelled, May 1960

APRIL 1961

Russian space
triumph

Yuri
Gagarin
first man into
orbit in space

Russians close off East Berlin,
August 1964

BERLIN WALL

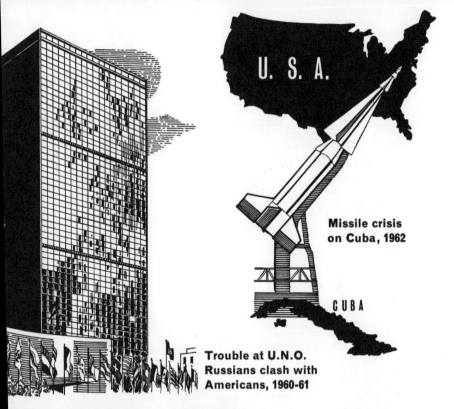

U.S.A.

Missile crisis
on Cuba, 1962

CUBA

Trouble at U.N.O.
Russians clash with
Americans, 1960-61

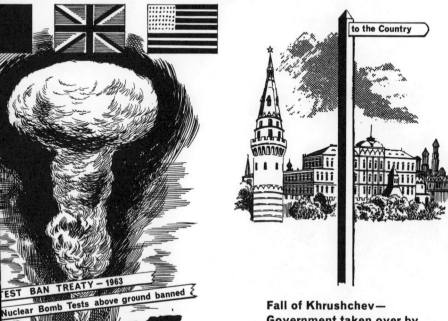

to the Country

TEST BAN TREATY – 1963
Nuclear Bomb Tests above ground banned

U.S.A., U.S.S.R. and Britain sign
Test-Ban Treaty, August 1963

Fall of Khrushchev—
Government taken over by
Brezhnev and Kosygin

Khrushchev and Cuba

From 1959 Soviet Russia had provided economic aid to Cuba and hinted at the provision of technical and military aid in addition. During 1962 Soviet military aid to Cuba included the setting up of Russian rocket missiles on the island. American reconnaissance planes brought back photographs of them in October 1962. President Kennedy put a naval blockade around Cuba and informed Russia that Soviet ships carrying missiles would be turned back. Fortunately for the world Khrushchev called his missiles home.

The Test-ban Treaty, August, 1963

Perhaps both the world leaders felt that they had come too close to the brink for safety. In June 1963 a special telephone line was opened between Washington and Moscow to provide direct personal telephone contact between the two leaders. Two months later a Test-ban treaty was signed by the U.S.A., Russia and Britain. The three nations agreed to give up nuclear bomb tests above ground and so lessen the growing danger of pollution of the atmosphere.

36   Alexei Nikolaevich Kosygin

37 Leonid Ilyich Brezhnev

The Fall of Khrushchev, October 1964

On October 16, 1964, it was announced from Moscow that Nikita Khrushchev had been released from his duties and that he had been replaced by Leonid Brezhnev as First Secretary and by Alexei Kosygin as Chairman of the Council of Ministers. Khrushchev had lost the support of the powerful Central Committee at a time when his popularity in the country was on the wane. In 1963 and 1964, Khrushchev's promises were being thrown back at him. The new consumer goods, the abundance of food, disarmament, better housing, none of these things so easily promised, had really materialised. The crisis over Cuba had caused Russia to lose face and the immense popularity of the space flights had died down in view of the shortages at home. His ambitious agricultural policy in Siberia and Kazakhstan, where millions of acres had been sown with wheat, ended in the disaster of the bad harvest and food shortage of 1963.

On October 12, 1964, the world's first multi-passenger spaceship, carrying three Russian cosmonauts, blasted off into space. The cosmonauts who were expecting to spend a week in space were ordered back to earth twenty-four hours later by the cryptic message: 'There are more things in heaven and earth than are dreamt of in your philosophy. Come down.' What the message meant was that the management of the Kremlin was about to be passed into new hands. This time it would not be Khrushchev who would stand by them on the dais to welcome the heroes of another Russian space triumph, for Khrushchev and his wife were on their way to the countryside and to the anonymity of private life.

Reading

The Romanovs *Almedingen*
A History of Russia *B. Pares*
The Bolshevik Revolution *E. H. Carr*
Stalin *I. Deutscher*
The Khrushchev Phase *A. Werth*
Unpersoned—The Fall of Nikita Khrushchev *Page and Burg*
The Soviet Union Today *Whiting*
History of U.S.S.R. *Avagon*

CHAPTER 10 *Work Programme*

A

1 Who was the last of the Czars?
2 What were the dates of his reign?
3 Who were the three major world powers at the beginning of the twentieth century?
4 Name the Russian dominions at the beginning of the twentieth century.
5 Why was the Czar so powerful?
6 On whom did he depend to carry out his policy?
7 What important work did Witte do?
8 What was the date of the Russo-Japanese War?
9 Who won the war?
10 Name three battles of the war.
11 What happened in St. Petersburg in 1905?
12 What concessions did the Czar make?
13 How many Dumas were held between 1906 and 1917?
14 What reforms were made by the Dumas?
15 When did the First World War break out?
16 Who were Russia's allies?
17 Whom did Russia fight against?
18 How did the war begin for Russia?
19 Who took over command of the Russian military forces in 1915?
20 Why was the war disastrous for the Czar?
21 What two revolutions broke out in Russia in 1917?

22 When did the Czar give up his throne?
23 When did the Czar and his family die?
24 How did they die?

B
1 Draw a sketch-map of the Russo–Japanese War.
2 Write your own account of the life of Nicholas II.
3 Write short notes on: the Russo–Japanese War, the Revolution of 1905, the Dumas, Russia and the First World War.

C
1 Could any Czar have saved the Russian Imperial régime during the years that were given to Nicholas II? How could it have been done?
2 'If Nicholas II was too weak to rule in the ruthless tradition of the Czars, Joseph Stalin was certainly not.' Compare the personalities and policies of these two rulers of Russia.

CHAPTER II   *Work Programme*

A
1   Why was 1917 an important year in Russian history?
2   Give three causes of the 'February' Revolution.
3   Where did the 'February' Revolution break out?
4   Why did the Czar abdicate?
5   Who was the leader of the new government?
6   What was the most powerful group behind the revolt?
7   Explain what a Soviet was.
8   Who controlled the Soviets in Petrograd?
9   Why did Kerensky become less popular?
10 Name three members of the Bolshevik Central Committee in 1917?
11 What did the Committee decide to do in October 1917?
12 Who organised the Bolshevik forces in 1917?
13 Give two results of the Revolution of 'October' 1917.
14 Who were the leaders of the new Bolshevik Government?
15 What happened to Kerensky?
16 What did Lenin do once the Bolsheviks had gained power?

17 What happened to the Czar?
18 Why was there Civil War in Russia between 1918–21?
19 Who guided the Bolshevik war effort?
20 Who built up the Red Army?
21 Explain the main features of 'War Communism'.
22 Who won the Civil War in Russia?
23 How did the Civil War affect Russia?
24 What changes in policy did Lenin make?
25 What features distinguished Communist Russia from other European nations?
26 Write down four reasons why the Russians remember Lenin.

B

1 Write a life story of Lenin.
2 Write short notes on: the 'February' and 'October' Revolutions, Kerensky, the Russian Civil War, 1918–21, Lenin's New Economic Policy.

C

1 Compare Lenin and Mao Tse-tung (see Book 2) as leaders of Communist Revolution.
2 'The most significant result of the First World War was the birth of Communist Russia.' Discuss.

CHAPTER 12 *Work Programme*

A

1 What was Joseph Stalin's home area?
2 What political doctrine interested him from an early age?
3 How did he try to spread socialist ideas in Russia?
4 In what area was he most active politically in his early years?
5 Where did he first meet Lenin and Trotsky?
6 What famous Bolshevik newspaper was he connected with?
7 Name the Bolshevik Committees of which he was a member in 1917.
8 What appointment gave Stalin his big chance to lead Russian Communism?

9   When did Lenin die?
10 Who were the two rivals for the leadership of Communist Russia?
11 What were Trotsky's qualifications for the leadership?
12 Why were Communist officials suspicious of Trotsky?
13 Why was Stalin considered a safer choice?
14 Show how Trotsky fell from power 1924–9.
15 What problem did Stalin face in the towns in 1929?
16 What was Stalin's solution to the grain shortage?
17 How did he reorganise Russian agriculture?
18 How were the Kulaks treated?
19 What did the collective farms achieve?
20 Why was the re-organisation of industry so important for Russia?
21 What special aspects of industry were most strongly developed in the nineteen-thirties?
22 Who controlled industrial production in Russia?
23 What means were used to increase production?
24 What do the letters U.S.S.R. stand for?
25 How many republics were included in the Soviet Union in 1924, 1939, 1966?
26 What do the terms (a) Soviet, (b) Socialist mean as included in the name of the Russian state?
27 Why is Russia a difficult country to govern?
28 What were the two most important Committees of early Communist régimes in Russia?
29 What gave Stalin his immense personal power?
30 What part did the Council of Commissars play in the government of Russia?
31 What part is played by the Communist Party in the Russian Government?
32 Name the two representative bodies introduced by the Constitution of 1936.
33 What has replaced the Politbureau in recent years in the Soviet Government?
34 What is the new name given to the Council of Commissars?
35 Name any two political leaders who have governed Russia since Stalin's death.

B

1   Write a life story of Joseph Stalin.

2 Draw a diagram to illustrate the main events in Russian history under Stalin.
3 Write short notes on: Trotsky, the collective farms, the Five Year Plans, the Government of the U.S.S.R.

C
Compare Hitler and Stalin as leaders of one-party states.

CHAPTER 13 *Work Programme*

A
1 Where and when was Khrushchev born?
2 When did he join the Communist Party?
3 What part did he play in the Russian Civil War?
4 Why was 1934 an important year for him?
5 What posts did he take up in 1944 and 1949?
6 Why was he in a strong position to take over from Stalin in 1953?
7 Why was the Second World War a triumph for Stalin?
8 How was the Russian position in Europe strengthened as the result of the war?
9 Why did co-operation between Russia and her wartime Allies break down after the war?
10 How did this lack of co-operation reach crisis point, 1948–9?
11 What do you understand by the term 'Cold War'?
12 In what ways did Russia make progress at home after the war?
13 Why was Stalin's government considered harsh?
14 When did Stalin die?
15 Who took over the government of Russia after his death?
16 When and why did Khrushchev win the final struggle for power in 1957?
17 In what ways did Khrushchev change Russian policy at home and abroad?
18 In what ways did Russian policy remain basically the same?
19 What was the crowning achievement of Khrushchev's career?
20 What upset Soviet–American relations in 1960?
21 What made these relations even worse during 1961?

22   Why was Khrushchev unwise in sending missiles to Cuba?
23   When did Khrushchev fall from power?
24   Give three reasons for his fall.
25   Who took over the government after Khrushchev?

B

1   Write short notes on the following: the Last Years of Stalin 1941–53, Khrushchev's Visit to the U.S.A. 1959, the Russian Space Programme, the Cuban Crisis 1962, the Test-ban Treaty 1963.
2   Write a short account of the early life of Khrushchev to 1953.
3   Outline the main events in Khrushchev's political career from 1953 to 1964.
4   Make a diagram to show the main events in the life of Khrushchev.

C

1   'Lenin laid the foundation stone but the building which emerged in later years was Stalin's.' Discuss this statement with reference to Twentieth Century Russia.
2   Show how Khrushchev gave a new twist to Russian policy at home and abroad while still maintaining the essential features of Russian Communist policy.
3   Ruthless power-seeker, disciple of Stalin, exponent of world peace and emancipator of Russia. Discuss the many-sided character of Khrushchev's political career.

Index

Acknowledgements

The author wishes to thank the following for permission to reproduce photographs:

United States Information Service, 1, 4, 5, 6, 7, 12, 17, 23, 25; Camera Press Ltd., 2, 3, 10, 13, 14, 15, 16, 18, 21, 26, 32, 33, 35, 36, 37; Radio Times Hulton Picture Library, 8, 11, 27, 28, 29, 30; Paul Popper Ltd., 9, 24; Keystone Press Agency Ltd., 19, 20, 22, 31, 34.